DEFENDO

DEFENDO

The Total Self-Defense System

Grips Self Protection Services Inc.

Macmillan of Canada

A Division of Gage Publishing Limited
Toronto, Canada

The right to use the Defendo name is owned
by Grips Self Protection Services Inc., and any
unauthorized attempt to teach this system of
self-defense for profit is prohibited.

Canadian Cataloguing in Publication Data
  Main entry under title:
  Defendo
  ISBN 0-7715-9758-4
  1. Self-defense.   I. Grips Self Protection Services.
  GV111.D43   613.6′6   C83-098100-4

Queries about Defendo can be addressed to:
Grips Self Protection Services Inc.
P.O. Box 689
Troy, MI 48099
United States of America
                OR
Grips Self Protection Services Inc.
Toronto, Ontario
Canada

Macmillan of Canada
A Division of Gage Publishing Limited

Cover & text design/Maher & Murtagh
Photography/Peter Paterson

Printed in Canada

Defendo is dedicated to
responsible and effective
self-defense

Acknowledgements

Grips Self Protection Services Inc. acknowledges with gratitude the assistance of the following:

Our special thanks to Harry van Bommel for coordinating this Defendo manual;

Our sincere thanks to Joseph N. Ferris for his guidance and understanding throughout the project;

Our thanks to Linda Press Fisher, our editor, and the entire staff at Macmillan of Canada, for their enthusiasm, professionalism, and efficiency;

Our thanks to John Murtagh, our designer, and Peter Paterson, our photographer, for the high quality of their work;

Our thanks to the following people for their help in preparing the manuscript: Stephen Campbell, Kathryn Ferris, Mike Hedley, Janet Klees, Daphne Simpson, Patrick D. Smith, Tom Warney, and Allen Wheaton, and also the Haas family, Philo van Enckevort, and the van Soest family;

Our thanks to the following models for their patient assistance: Anna Ferris, Kathryn Ferris, Josi Perotto, Barbara and Robert Rochard, Rory Sheehan, John and Harry van Bommel, and Allen Wheaton;

Our special thanks to John van Bommel, without whose encouragement and support this manual would not have been completed on time;

Our special thanks also to Janet Klees for her belief in this project and her support throughout.

DEFENDO

Contents

INTRODUCTION

Defendo is learned for protection, not domination.

You are walking down a well-lit street towards your apartment building when you glance back and notice that a man who was staring at you on the bus home has got off at the same stop and is walking a short distance behind you down the same street. You casually cross the road to the other side. You hear the unmistakable sound of his footsteps also crossing the road.

You are standing against the wall at a party when a large and slightly drunk man trips near you and spills his entire drink over your shoes. You protest indignantly and he steps right up to you, grabs your shirt, and pushes you again and again against the wall.

These are not exaggerated nightmares, to be brushed away as hysterical and paranoid. Nor are they scenarios that should make you afraid of venturing out of your house alone. They are descriptions of violent encounters which occur frequently in streets and homes across North America, but against which you can learn to defend yourself.

Escalating violent crime rates in North America make it practical to learn a form of self-defense which can be used by anyone, regardless of sex, age, body stature, or physical fitness. Defendo is such a system. It was first developed by William J. Underwood, who studied jiujitsu at the beginning of the century with the Japanese masters Tara Maki and Jukio Tani. By the time the Second World War broke out, Underwood had developed his system sufficiently to teach Canadian and American armed forces the "Combato" method of unarmed combat. Eventually a purely defensive system was developed and named Defendo. Since then, Defendo has been taught to police, security personnel, public transportation staff, and shift workers; it has been adapted for pregnant women, senior citizens, handicapped people, and those suffering from back problems and other physical ailments.

How does Defendo work? It is based on two principles: the application of sudden piercing pain to specific pressure points on the body, and the use of the attacker's strength and momentum to the defender's advantage. Even if completely outmatched in terms of muscle power and size, any victim has a good chance of defense if he or she has studied and practiced a variety of Defendo moves.

However, Defendo is not designed to help you become a hero, conquer the world, or beat up an argumentative acquaintance. It is a last resort only, a method of defending yourself with physical force if there is no alternative. If there is the threat of a violent encounter, first try talking in a calm voice; then try being cooperative up to a reasonable point (by giving up your wallet and jewelry, for example); and then try to escape safely. If you succeed, you will have learned Defendo's key lesson. Avoiding a confrontation means you have *won* the confrontation.

If you *have* to defend yourself, then you should be well prepared. The keys to the proper use of this book and to your own safety are simple:

Think about potentially dangerous situations that could arise. You can do this while you drive to work, ride a public transport system, walk to the store, or watch a thriller on television. Ask yourself, "What would I do if that person tried to assault me in a certain situation? What would I do if ...?"

Talk about these situations with your family, friends, neighbors, and colleagues. Compare your solutions with theirs.

Plan ahead for situations, so that if someone bothers you on the bus or an acquaintance at a New Year's Eve party pays you unwelcome and persistent attention, you already have a rough plan to follow.

Practice for these situations. This is perhaps the most important principle to follow, for one needs conditioned reflexes to counter serious assaults. Although it becomes an automatic reaction to slam on the brakes if a child seems about to dart out in front of your car, that response is only learned through practice. Thinking about what you will do if there is a fire in your home is important, but unless your family has actually practiced a plan of action there will be confusion and panic which could be fatal. The practice sessions for Defendo should be seen as stimulating and fun. Involve friends who are visiting in the evening, neighbors having a barbecue in the backyard, bored teenagers, or your colleagues at work. While you make a game of the practice session, you will also be preparing to respond automatically and effectively in a real-life attack.

PREVENTIVE SUGGESTIONS

Crimes are committed against the vulnerable, not the prepared.

Why are so many people apathetic about learning self-protection? Perhaps the most common reason is fear. They are reluctant to think about the likelihood of an attack and the trauma they would experience, so they never face the subject directly and practically. Others are too busy to worry about potential dangers. Too often they shrug: "It could never happen to me." But North American statistics show that each one of us is likely to be attacked and/or robbed at least once in a lifetime. Another reason many people will never read about or practice a method of self-defense is that they feel it is melodramatic or hysterical to worry about assaults, robberies, or rape. But *Defendo* was not written to make its readers paranoid or to instill fear about going out or meeting new people. On the contrary, a knowledge of basic self-defense and a developed habit of awareness promote self-confidence and reassurance.

We all subject ourselves to risk, either consciously or unconsciously. Women working late in deserted offices take the risks involved in riding the elevator, waiting for the subway, and walking home alone, because they *have* to, for practical reasons. But if you do nothing else to protect yourself, at least start being aware of and alert to your surroundings. Your senses and intuition are your own private warning

alarms, so pay attention to your hunches and premonitions. Many victims of crimes have had a "gut feeling" that something was unusual and wrong in their environment, but they ignored their own warnings. Only those who ignore their instincts find out whether they were wrong or not, and by then it is too late.

Take note of the following preventive suggestions, and then try the awareness quiz that follows.

While Walking on the Street

General suggestions

1. The most important rule when walking alone or with others is to *walk assertively*. Keep your head up, maintain a brisk and steady pace, and be aware of your surroundings.
2. Avoid walking alone at night in poorly lit, isolated streets and high-crime areas. This advice has been repeated again and again, but it is all too often ignored, resulting in thousands of attacks and robberies yearly in those same areas.
3. Always carry "emergency money" for a phone call and, if possible, for a cab ride. Never use this money for anything else. However, in most cities, emergency numbers (police, fire, ambulance) are free.
4. Always carry your keys in your

hand, even if you are just going for a casual stroll, with the key you will need next between your thumb and index finger. This is necessary to save time if you are threatened and need to get into your house or car quickly. A key is also a good weapon when held this way. It can be used to slash an attacker across his face, to strike various pressure points that you will learn about in the next chapter, or even to throw into his face to divert his hands (his automatic reaction will be to try to catch the keys) while you strike or kick him and escape. Many women place a key between each finger of the stronger hand, so that four keys on a key ring are sticking out of a tight fist. But this can work against you, because if your hand is caught and squeezed, the pain is excruciating.

Protecting your handbag or camera case

5. Avoid carrying a handbag for short trips to the store or post office. Keep some cash and your keys in a front pocket where you can place your arm or hand on top of it casually without looking suspicious.
6. If you do carry a handbag, use a small one and tuck it under your arm. If it has a shoulder strap, use it even while you have the purse tucked securely under your arm. Avoid carrying a bag loosely in your hand or hanging freely from your shoulder.

7. If the bag opens along the side, have that side next to your body under your arm.

8. Avoid public displays of large amounts of money. Many purse-snatchers wait outside banks, post offices, and busy stores at Christmas time.

9. If someone tries to take your purse, *do not fight*. Personal property is not worth the risk of injury. Only if you are in physical danger should you use force.

10. If your purse is stolen, yell for help (if the robber cannot hurt you to stop you from doing so), note what he looks like, and watch to see where he goes (or follow him at a safe distance while you continue yelling).

11. Report the crime to the police immediately and tell them as many details as you can remember.

If you suspect danger

12. In a quiet street, walk in the middle of the road. On a busier street, always walk on the curb side of the sidewalk (unless there are occupied cars along the side). These measures will give you more warning if an assailant runs out from a hiding place between buildings, in dark alleyways or door entrances, or behind bushes. However, if there is a car parked along the curb with passengers inside and you feel uneasy, cross the street to the opposite side or move closer to the inner side of the sidewalk for that short space.

13. Always try to walk on the side of the road where you will be facing oncoming traffic. This makes it more difficult for a car to follow you closely.

14. If you are asked for directions by someone in a car, stay clear of the doors, keep your answer short, and move on.

15. If you are approached by a stranger requesting information or assistance, give him a short answer and move on. If you are suspicious of his motives, ignore his question, walk away, and report him to the police.

16. If you are accosted by an exhibitionist, ignore him and contact the police. You should not make any comment or laugh, as he may become violent. Turn around and hurry away.

17. If you suspect that you are being followed, turn around and look at your pursuer. If a criminal sees that you are observant and prepared, he is likely to want to find an easier victim. It is a good idea to do a quick 360-degree turn every few minutes when you are walking alone in a quiet area. You will thus become aware of anyone following you, and also show him that you are alert.

Escaping

18. If he continues to follow you, cross over the street. If he crosses too, you have several alternatives. Put yourself in a position where there is a parked car between you and him and scream for help. The attention you draw may persuade him that you are not worth the risk. Too many women are embarrassed about creating a disturbance even when they suspect danger, and delay too long before they call for help. You can also walk toward someone else and explain that you think you are being followed and would he mind talking to you for a few minutes or walking you to safety. Most people are aware of such situations and are glad to help as long as they do not feel threatened themselves. Use your head and keep calm. Another alternative is to run towards a store that is open or a lighted house.

19. Do not run directly home if you can avoid doing so, as this will show your pursuer where you live and you will always be concerned about his waiting for you there again.

20. Except when your assailant is armed with a gun or in a good position to quiet you forcefully, it is important that you scream for help. Even if it is unlikely that anyone will hear, there is always that possibility, and anyway your noise will confuse and concern the person threatening you. Shout "Fire!" or "Police!" rather than "Help! Rape!" as people are more likely to run to investigate. This also reminds them to phone the police even if they don't want to

become involved personally.

21. If you are running away, kick off your shoes if you can run more quickly without them. The other advantage of this is that your pursuer will not be able to hear your footsteps if you are trying to hide.
22. Run in a straight line so that your pursuer cannot cut you off.
23. Do not look back, as this slows yo down. Rather, listen for this footsteps.
24. If you find a hiding place, remain perfectly still. Do not peek out to see if he is still around as he may be waiting quietly for you to reveal yourself. Wait as long as you feel you can bear, plus ten minutes, before coming out and seeking help, in case your pursuer doubles back and comes to look for you again.

The buddy system

25. If you live alone, try to establish a buddy system with friends or neighbors to do your shopping or laundry together.
26. When meeting a group of people for a social gathering or meeting, tr to arrange a car pool or take a taxi together.
27. If several people have brought cars to a function and have parked them in various locations, it is safest to walk together to the nearest car and then drop off each person at his or her car. Your security is well worth the effort.

Store Robberies

1. There is a definite increase in the number of public robberies in banks and stores, and you may be in a store one day and witness such a situation. If you are in your own store and someone suspicious enters, phone a spouse or a friend and ask them to stay on the phone until the customer leaves.
2. In a hold-up situation, follow all orders without hesitation or sudden movements.
3. Do not assume that there is only one robber. The chances are that there is another one at the door, outside, or in the getaway car.
4. If the robbers are unmasked, do not stare at them. Trying to note their description so obviously will only anger them.
5. If shooting begins, fall to the floor immediately. Be completely silent and lie motionless with your face down. Any attempt to be a hero could seriously endanger other people's lives.
6. *Never use force to protect property.* It is not worth physical injury.

Car Safety

When parking your car

1. The most important rule is *always lock your car*, whether you are inside or out.
2. Glance *under* your car as you walk up to it. Assailants have been known to hide underneath and grab the driver's ankles as she unlocks the door.
3. Always glance at the floor behind your seat before you get into your car.
4. Park your car in an attended lot or a well-lit or busy area. If you have to park in an isolated garage, drive around the area first to check that you are completely alone and park as close as possible to the exit. If you see someone lurking near by in a suspicious manner, do not leave your car. It is a very safe haven. If you are in your own apartment building, drive away and phone the superintendent or a friend to meet you in the garage and escort you home.
5. When loading your trunk with packages, have the driver's door open in case you need to get in quickly. Be alert. If someone approaches your car, get in, lock the doors, and wait to see what the person wants.
6. When getting into your car loaded down with packages, get in as quickly as possible and lock the door first. Then take the time to arrange your packages, coat, or groceries properly.
7. If you are in a parked car and need help, blow your horn. The Morse code signal for help is simply three short honks, three long ones, and then three short ones again (S.O.S.), and it is well known to most people.

If your car breaks down

8. Keep your car in good running order; it is dangerous to risk a possible breakdown when you are alone.

9. If you are stranded on the highway, lift the car's hood, return to your car, lock the doors, put on your hazard light and, if possible, your inside light, close your windows except for a little space to let fresh air in, and wait for the highway police or the Motor League patrol. If you can start the car regularly for a few minutes for warmth, continue to do so.

10. If someone stops to help you, do not get out of the car but ask him to notify the nearest service station or police department. There is a chance that someone offering to help you may have ulterior motives. Offer them the chance to help by making a phone call for you and thank them for their assistance. Even if they become persistent or get upset by your apparent "rudeness," do not leave your car or let them in.

11. If you are stranded on a secondary road and you can see a lighted house near by from which you could phone a service station, raise the hood, lock the car behind you, and walk to the house. Always be very alert to your surroundings.

12. If you have a flat tire and feel unsafe about getting out of the car, drive very slowly with your hazard lights on. You may ruin the tire, but you will be safe.

If your car is being followed

13. If you suspect that you are being followed by another car, drive immediately to the nearest service station, restaurant, police station, fire hall, or hospital. Blow your horn to attract attention.

14. If you are being followed on a highway or a multi-lane road, keep to the left lane, as it is more difficult to cut somone off from this lane — any attempt to do so would be clearly visible (if not a traffic hazard!) to other drivers.

If someone tries to get into your car forcibly

15. If someone tries to get into your car forcibly at a stop sign or a red light, blow your horn to attract attention and drive away quickly. Your doors should *always* be locked and your windows should be closed or open only slightly.

16. If someone is trying to force you out of your car by standing in front of it, drive forward slowly in low gear (for maximum power and least likelihood of stalling) and then pick up speed.

17. If a gang lifts the back of your car or bounces you up and down, gun the accelerator to enable you to drive away.

18. If someone puts his hand in through the window and you roll up the window to catch it there, or if he breaks a hole in the window and reaches through to grab you, you are in a good position to hit his hand against the broken glass or to strike or burn it with a flashlight or flare from your glove compartment. Keep your hand on your horn.

19. After you have escaped, report the incident to the police immediately.

If someone manages to get into the car with you

20. If an unarmed person forces his way into your car, quickly take your keys out of the ignition and get out of the car yourself if possible.

21. If an unarmed person has forced his way into your car and is ordering you to go somewhere, try to judge whether or not he is familiar with the area; if he seems not to be, drive to the nearest police station, fire hall, hospital, construction site, or place of activity to get help.

22. If the person is armed and your life is in immediate danger, you must take a greater chance. As you drive, try to think clearly and plan ahead. You may decide to hit a building or a large snow bank, or even just to make a sudden stop.

23. If a gunman in the car is threatening to kill you, speed up so that killing you would also kill him. Blow your horn while driving very, very fast to attract attention, preferably that of the police. Drive directly to a police station — the gunman's options are limited if he wants to stop you.

Valuables in your car

24. Do not leave valuables in clear sight in the car. Lock them in the trunk or hide them under the seat.
25. Put identification numbers on your valuables, such as a tape deck, and keep a record in case accessories are stolen. Check with your local police for information on any identification program they may have.
26. If your car is broken into, do not touch the door handles or anything else. Call the police immediately. If the break-in occurred outside your home, check with the neighbors in case there were any witnesses.

Public Transportation

1. Know the bus and train schedules so that you do not have to wait longer than is necessary.
2. While waiting for a bus or a train, be aware of your surroundings. Do not fall asleep in bus, train, or plane terminals.
3. Avoid waiting inside shelters where you can be trapped.
4. Have the proper change ready for your ticket so that you do not display more money than is absolutely necessary. Use a separate change purse if possible.
5. Always try to sit near the driver, conductor, or motorman. It is safer to sit next to a woman than a man. Always try to find an aisle seat from which you can get up quickly. (This is also true for cinemas and theaters.)
6. Try to sit in a train or subway car where there are other people. Should most or all of them exit, move to another car. There is generally safety in numbers.
7. Hold onto your briefcase, purse, or packages. This will discourage a potential thief and prevent you from leaving them behind.
8. If someone bothers you verbally or physically, leave immediately and report it to the driver or the conductor. Do not continue a conversation with someone who is harassing you. This is also true for a "friendly drunk" — avoid him without necessarily being rude.
9. If traveling alone at night, ask someone to pick you up at your destination, or at least warn someone of your expected time of arrival so that your non-arrival will cause concern.
10. If, upon leaving a bus or train, you feel that someone is following you, try to return to the vehicle or the station, or run to a nearby business, restaurant, or occupied house. Do not lead him to your residence.

Hitchhiking

1. Hitchhiking is extremely dangerous. However, for economic reasons, some people who leave their jobs in the middle of the night, and cannot afford a taxi, do hitchhike. If your employer will not provide transportation and you cannot form a car pool with other employees, we strongly recommend that you follow these suggestions to minimize the danger of hitchhiking. Keep in mind at all times, however, that there is a very real need for you to be alert. Remember that hitchhiking includes getting a lift with *anyone* you don't know well, even if you have chatted with that person for an evening in a bar, or if you have a mutual acquaintance.
2. Accept a ride only if there is a single person (preferably a woman or a senior citizen) in the car, or a man-and-woman couple. Do not accept rides when there are two or more men.
3. Do not accept a ride immediately. Talk to the person and look to see if the doors have inside handles on them. Make sure the locks are not controlled by the driver alone. Do not be afraid to refuse a ride.
4. Do not get into the back seat of a car if there is someone already there. Your chances of escape from this position are slight.
5. If there is a single occupant, sit in the front where you are in a

position to grab the steering wheel and possibly the brake, after defending yourself against him. You can also see his movements more clearly.

6. If there is a couple in the front seat, sit behind the driver, to avoid having the passenger in the front grab you should you need to escape.

7. If you sense danger at all, calmly and carefully plan your escape. The car must stop at some time. Carry in your hand your keys or some other object which you can use as a weapon. When the opportunity presents itself, open the door and run away quickly. If escape is not possible without a confrontation, be prepared mentally and physically.

8. When accepting a ride, ask the driver's destination before giving your own. If he refuses, do not accept the ride. In fact, never allow yourself to be driven directly to your home or business but get out at a neutral site.

At Home Alone

General tips

1. Always draw the curtains or blinds at night to prevent people outside from seeing if you are alone and from studying your personal habits.

2. It is a good idea to have lights on in various rooms of your home.

Along with the sound of a radio or TV, this signals to someone outside that there are a number of people home.

3. When sleeping at night, leave a light on in the kitchen or the bathroom to indicate that someone is up late. This discourages "brave" burglars who will only rob your home while you are sleeping.

4. A dog is one of the best ways to protect yourself and your home. Statistics indicate that the size of the dog is not important. More important is that the dog makes a lot of noise when he senses something unusual. All other weapons — guns, spray cans, baseball bats, etc. — can be taken away and used against you, or else they may be in another part of the house when you are robbed or attacked.

Know your neighborhood

5. When you move into a new home, check the following points:
   a) the address and location of local police and fire stations
   b) the direct phone number of your local police division
   c) police recommendations for safety precautions in your area
   d) where outdoor pay phones are located
   e) which stores, restaurants, and gas stations are open late, so that you could ask for assistance in an emergency

6. Participate in or encourage the

development of Block Parent programs and Neighborhood Watch plans. Statistics show that when neighbors cooperate in such programs, crime decreases in that area. The local police department will assist you to set up such a program if none exists.

7. Do not give out information about your neighbors to anyone you do not know — for example, that the neighbor lives alone or is on vacation. Anyone can pose as an insurance salesman, a service man, an investigator, or a long-lost cousin.

Security improvements for your home

8. All entrances, garages, and pathways between the garage and the entrance to your home should be well-lit to discourage lurkers. Leave these outdoor lights on all night to discourage anyone from hiding on your property or using the dark to cover a break-in into your home. Your neighbors should be able to see your doors and windows clearly, so keep your hedges trimmed.

9. The house number should be large, clear, and visible from the road so that emergency vehicles can locate your home easily.

10. Doors should be equipped with a peep-hole to allow you to see clearly who is outside. These are not too expensive to install, considering their value every time

the doorbell rings. Chains are no substitute, as the screws attaching them to the door frame can be pulled out with a hard kick or blow to the door.

11. Outside doors should be solid with a one-inch deadbolt lock, available in most hardware stores. An auxiliary rim-mounted lock with a deadbolt is a very good supplementary lock. Buy a tapered deadbolt, as this is hard to wrench from its socket. If it has any external screws, distort the heads.

12. Outside doors should be equipped with a mail slot to allow the passage of small packages and mail. This is also necessary when you want to verify the identification of tradesmen or policemen. However, your mail slot should be covered from within so that no one can look through the slot into your home.

13. Windows and sliding doors must also be protected with locks. You can regulate the opening width of windows and sliding doors by placing a broomstick or similar object in the track runner so that an intruder would have to break the glass to get in. Place screws in the sliding track at the top of windows or doors to prevent a burglar from lifting them out of the track completely. Check with your local police for more information.

Valuables

14. Check with the local police department about inscribing identification numbers on your valuables. Keep a list of these, of serial numbers, and of all your unmarked valuables in your bank safety deposit box; otherwise it will be difficult for you to reclaim your stolen items.

15. All original copies of important papers such as birth certificates, stocks and bonds, and passports should be kept in your safety deposit box. Photocopies of documents which you have to keep on your person — driver's license, credit cards, and health insurance, for example — should be kept in the deposit box too.

Keys

16. Never hide your keys in a "secret" place outside your home, as any experienced burglar will have heard of every place you can think of. Rather, give a spare key to a trusted neighbor.

17. If you lose your keys, you should change all the outside locks immediately. You may have dropped them conspicuously near your house, and the person who finds them will have no trouble in getting in. Do not attach personal identification to your key chain; rather, attach a note suggesting that the finder hand them in to the police or send them to your postal box number if you have one.

18. Do not leave your house keys with a repair or parking garage — take only the key they will need off your key chain. Do not leave a spare house key in or attached magnetically to your car; if your car is stolen, the thief may also trace and rob your house.

Telephone safety

19. Before going to sleep tonight, attach a directory of the following numbers to your phone in large printed letters and numbers: police, fire department, ambulance, doctor, poison control, rape crisis center, and other important numbers, including your place of employment should another household member need to reach you. In case your mind goes blank in an emergency, write down your own address and phone number. Whenever notifying police of immediate danger, give your address first in case you don't have time to give more information.

20. When speaking on the phone to a stranger, never say that you are alone. If you are suspicious of a call for one of the other household members, say that he is busy at the moment but will call back as soon as possible.

21. If you receive a "wrong number" call, do not give out your own number. If the caller wants to be sure that it really is a wrong number, ask what the desired number is and indicate that it is incorrect.

22. Use only your initial(s) with your name in the phone directory, in any advertisement notices, in

bulletin-board listings, or on your mail box. Never use your full name to indicate your sex or that you live alone.

Obscene telephone calls

23. Do not respond at all. *Hang up* immediately and notify the police at once. Although the police cannot do anything immediately, if more people report such calls, a pattern may be discovered and the caller arrested.
24. If the caller persists, contact your phone company and if necessary change your number or maintain an unlisted number.
25. If these calls persist, keep a log of each call: the date, time, caller's approximate age and sex, background noises, and any exact language used. This will aid the phone company and the police in their investigation.
26. Do not assume that it is just some youngster playing a prank. These calls can be serious and should be treated as such.

When someone comes to the door

27. Ask who is there before opening the door. Keep in mind as well that just because someone knocks at your door you are not obligated to answer.
28. Look through a peep-hole in your door to see who is there. If someone has put a finger over it or is too close for you to see who it is, ask him to move back. Even if it is just an expected friend playing

"an innocent joke," do not make any assumptions.

29. Ask for identification if it is a service representative, a policeman, or a salesman. If he does not have it or refuses to slip the identification under the door or through the mail box, do not let him in.
30. In the case of a service representative, ask for his office number, verify it with the phone book, and call to make sure that the "gas man" or the "phone company rep" is there for the reason he states. This all takes time, but uniforms can be rented and fake cards printed, so a proper check is necessary.
31. If you should open your door and someone tries to push it open further, keep your foot flat on the floor with your toes pushed up against the bottom of the door. This will make it more difficult to rip a chain from the doorframe and is a very effective doorstop in an emergency. Try it and see.
32. Call the police if a person demands entrance with any aggressiveness at all.

If there is a burglar on your property

33. If you see someone suspicious around your own home or the home of a neighbor, do not hesitate to call the police. Do not assume that someone else has already notified the police.
34. Do not think you are paranoid

if you suspect someone is inside or outside. Instincts are very important and are often reliable. Over a long period you will have become familiar with the different noises around your home, so you may well be right to be concerned if you hear something unusual.

35. If you suspect someone is outside your home, do not go out to check. Call the police immediately. If it is dark outside, check that all your outdoor lights and a few indoor lights are on. Do not allow your silhouette to be seen as you do this.
36. If you wake up to see a burglar in your house, pretend to be asleep. He will probably not harm you if he thinks he can take what he wants and escape.
37. If a prowler enters your home when you are near an exit, escape if you can and call the police from a neighbor's home. Practice an escape plan — like a fire drill — with your family.
38. Some homes have "safe rooms" in case of an emergency. These can be a bathroom or a closet equipped with a strong door, a deadbolt lock, and an unlisted telephone line separate from your house line. If you sense danger in your home, lock yourself in your "safe room" and phone the police.
39. Some homes have silent and loud alarms connected to the local police station. Ask the police for advice on the appropriate alarm.
40. If escape is impossible, remain

calm and cooperative. Try to note a clear description of the thief and remember if he touches anything with his bare hands, thus leaving fingerprints. If you can get a description of his get-away car, its license number, and the direction in which he drove, repeat them aloud as soon as he leaves and then write them down immediately. Lock all the doors in case he returns, and phone the police. While you wait for them, do not disturb anything, but jot down any details and descriptions you can remember.

41. If you arrive home to find that your house has been broken into, do not enter. The burglar may still be inside or you may disturb evidence the police will need. Go to a neighbor or a store to phone the police.

Elevators

42. When you are in an elevator, stand by the controls and face the other people, especially if there are only two or three passengers. This will help prevent someone from surprising you or stopping the elevator between floors. If necessary, use the emergency alarm button to signal for help by pushing it continuously, or preferably by using the S.O.S. signal. Also push several floor buttons quickly so that you can get out at the first opportunity or scream every time the door opens.

43. If other passengers get on at the same time and you are unsure of them, let them push their floor buttons first and then push a button of a floor higher up. That way they do not know which floor you live on, they get off first, and you can safely go to your proper floor alone.

44. If someone suspicious gets on the elevator, do not be hesitant about getting off yourself and waiting for the next one.

45. Make sure that if you are going up, the elevator is not going down to the basement first. Wait until an elevator is going in the same direction as you are.

Apartment lobbies, mail rooms, and laundry rooms

46. Do not let strangers into your apartment building by using the intercom system from your apartment or by opening the lobby door with your own key.

47. If you find yourself in trouble in an apartment lobby and you are near the intercom board, push as many buttons as you can to ask for help. Sometimes just leaning against the board will be sufficient to scare someone away.

48. In apartment buildings, always take your mail to your apartment immediately rather than going through it in the mail room. While you are sorting it in the mail room your concentration will be so fixed on your mail that you will not be aware of your surroundings and any strangers near by.

49. Avoid being alone in an apartment laundry room. Put your clothes in the machine and return later when they are ready.

Workmen in your home

50. If there is a plumber or a carpenter working in your home, do not offer social conversation or have coffee breaks together. If you choose to offer him coffee or a cold drink, put it in the room where he is working and leave him to continue with his job. Remain businesslike at all times.

51. Do not state that you are alone. If this is obvious, make a phone call and mention that there is a workman in your home, or make some excuse to tell him casually that you expect a visitor soon.

52. Practice separating sounds in your home and identifying them. That way you are less likely to be frightened by the refrigerator motor starting or the noisy pipes clanging. When you hear an unexpected sound, such as a workman walking to your bedroom when he is supposed to be working in the kitchen, you will hear it more easily and be on the alert. There is no need to be paranoid, but you should always be alert.

53. If a workman makes any advances, say "No" very assertively and call a friend. If he is persistent, leave the house immediately and call the police and his superiors. If you cannot

escape, lock yourself in a room, yell out the window for help, and call the police if there is a phone in the room.

When leaving on vacation

54. Have someone drop in regularly to keep the grounds neat, check the inside of your home, water the plants, and collect your mail or any newspapers you may have forgotten to cancel. Having a neighbor park in your driveway occasionally is also an indication that someone is home.

55. Draw the curtains and blinds only part way before you leave and ask your neighbor or friend to change the positions of the drapes and blinds occasionally.

56. Have lights, radio, and TV turned on in the evenings with timers you can buy in most hardware stores. This is useful even if you are out only for an evening.

57. Do not tell too many people that you are going out for the evening or on vacation, and for how long.

58. Lock *all* doors and windows to prevent easy access while you are away. Most burglaries occur through *unlocked* doors and windows (even on second or third floors). Do not assume that balcony doors even on the highest floors of apartment buildings are burglar-proof.

59. Have a house-sitter if you will be gone for an extended time.

60. Contact your newspaper office and any other regular delivery service to cut off service. Do not inform them that you are going on vacation or when you would like service reinstated. Call them when you return.

61. Let a neighbor or a police officer know where they can reach you in an emergency. Also let them know when you expect to be back, so that if something occurs on your vacation, your neighbor will notify the police that you have not returned. Give your neighbor a key to your home in case of an emergency.

62. If you suspect that someone with a spare key will enter your home (on a visit unauthorized by you) while you are away, attach a small piece of tape from door to frame or place a small folded piece of paper at the bottom of your door. If it has been moved or is gone, someone has been in your home. If necessary, call the police.

If You Are Attacked by Two or More People

1. If you can talk yourself out of such a situation or escape, do so.

2. Build up your anger until it overrides your fear. You will probably be hit by at least one of your attackers and you must be experiencing enough anger at that time to ignore the pain and concentrate on defending yourself with determination and rage.

3. Try to put a car, a table, or a tree between you and your opponents while you keep talking to distract them. If you can get your back against a wall or a large object (such as the side of a truck), you will have cut their field of attack by half. They must then come in from the front or side only and cannot attack your back. Use the wall for balance and maintain a firm stance.

4. Concentrate your attention on the leader of the group. The others may give up if their spokesman is on the ground in pain.

5. Pretend to concentrate on one person to trick the one you have really chosen to come close to you. Watch him from the corner of your eye and as he comes very close, kick or strike hard and yell *loudly*.

6. If there are three or more, try to hurt one of the people on the end first. If you knock down the middle person, the two end people will come together. If you knock down someone at the end, you can put his body on the ground between yourself and the rest of the group.

7. If you are not able to move against a wall and one person comes up behind you and one in front of you, one possibility is to step back quickly and forcefully into the opponent behind you. This will surprise him and he will probably grab onto you for support. While

he tries to regain his balance, kick the knee or shin of the person coming forward towards you with all your strength. Then hit or kick the person behind you.

8. Strike with all your might in this kind of attack. If you kick a knee, the cartilage must tear and the knee break. If you hit an elbow, the joint must snap.

9. Yell forcefully, using swear words, to increase your own anger and intimidate your attackers. Yell each time you strike a point.

10. The element of surprise is with you as your attackers will have expected you to be frightened by their numbers. If you strike rapidly again and again, they will not be able to react quickly enough to resist you effectively.

11. Escape as soon as you can, in case you are unable to beat your attackers again.

Gun Assaults

1. If you are threatened by an assailant with a gun, determine his motive by asking what he wants. His answer may help you plan your defense. If he wants your valuables, give him everything he asks for immediately. Do not startle him with sudden movements, but tell him exactly what you are doing, like "Now I am reaching for my wallet."

2. Cooperate fully unless your doing so will get you into further danger, like getting into a car. But this is a judgement you will only be able to make at that time.

3. If you have a chance to run, remember that most people are not experienced handgun users, especially at night. It takes many hours of practice to be able to use a handgun effectively. If you try to escape, run quickly in a zigzag movement.

4. If the gunman is nervous and inexperienced, there is always the danger that he will fire accidentally. Without moving your feet, twist slowly to the side from the hip upwards to move your upper body out of the gun's line. Keep talking at all times (unless this seems to irritate the gunman) and watch the gun. Practice this movement with a friend.

5. If the gun discharges, pretend to be hit and lie motionless. He may run away in fear and shock.

6. Even if you are hit, do not give up. You may still be able to fight back.

7. Another technique is to fake a faint, collapse, or seizure. This unexpected reaction will confuse and panic him and he may run away.

Rape

1. Do you resist or not? There is no pat answer for this difficult question. A woman must decide for herself whether to resist or not, depending on the circumstances and her ability to physically defend herself. She must know how to resist if she decides to do so.

2. Rape defence options are:
   a) choosing not to resist the attack if you fear for your own life and the lives of family members or others also held captive;
   b) passive resistance by trying to talk to the rapist to calm him and play for time.
   c) active resistance — *be prepared and proficient*. If you are hesitant to hurt the man who is raping you and perhaps will kill you, then you have lost. Therefore, it is imperative that you learn a form of self-defense, practice it, discuss it with others, and become accustomed to the prospect of having to hurt someone to save yourself.

3. If you choose not to resist at all:
   a) pretend to faint — there is a possibility that he may be dissuaded by your total lack of response;
   b) try to remain calm and in control mentally, although obviously this is very difficult;
   c) try to relax the pelvic area;
   d) do not complain or beg;

e) do not threaten revenge;

f) obtain a description if possible;

g) note the direction in which he flees;

h) if you choose to report the attack to the police, you may want to call a rape crisis center first. A counsellor will accompany you to the police station and hospital and give you support and advice on the legal system. This is best done as soon as possible.

i) if possible, do not change your clothes or wash before you are examined.

4. If you decide to resist, do something immediately and do not hold back.

5. As most rapists are known to their victims, loud and vigorous resistance is unexpected. Scream, be verbally aggressive, hit and kick with all your strength.

6. In some cases, it is effective to talk to a rapist calmly and choose the moment when you consider he is weakest — then put all your force into defending yourself and escaping.

7. Even if you choose not to report the incident to the police, call a rape crisis center or a friend for assistance. Do not keep the pain and humiliation of the attack to yourself. Crisis centers are located in almost every city and they will not even ask for your name if you do not wish to give it.

8. Remember that, no matter the circumstances, if you are raped, you are an innocent victim. There is no more reason to feel guilt than if you had been the victim of any other violent crime.

9. Teenaged girls who are babysitting should not open the front door for anyone they do not know well, even if the visitors claim to be relations or friends. Call home some time during the evening to confirm that everything is all right; if you do not call within a certain hour, your parents could call you and then come over to see what is wrong. Do not walk home alone in the dark — the people for whom you are babysitting should escort or drive you home. If you do not know them well, ask a friend or your parents to pick you up.

10. Several false but common beliefs on the subject of rape can be disproved by the following statistics on rapes in the United States:*

a) Most rapes are a complete surprise to the victim, but at least 40 percent of the victims know or are acquainted with the rapist and most rapes occur in the victim's home.

b) Almost all rape victims fear that they will be killed, but only about 5 percent of victims are actually killed and most victims do not suffer serious physical injury. Weapons are used in over half of all rapes.

c) Women often fear that their rapist will try to attack them again, but this almost never happens.

d) Most rapists plan their attacks, but it is not true that they go after pretty young women.

e) Most rapists are employed and have at least a high school education.

f) Most rapists are repeat offenders who have also committed robberies and assaults before.

g) Most rapists have a normal sexual outlet such as a wife or girlfriend. Rape is an act of violence against women rather than a sexual expression.

*Statistics taken from the National Crime Prevention Test, NBC Network, 1982.

Battered Wives

This is far too complex a problem to be covered in this brief chapter; it involves the financial dependence of many women on their husbands, the emotional burdens of shame and fear, the reluctance and helplessness of the authorities to interfere in "family matters," the isolation of non-English-speaking women, and still-powerful notions of male domination. However, a few points are offered in the hope that they may help in some small measure.

1. Do not believe your husband or boyfriend when he says that it will never happen again. Statistics indicate strongly that if it happened once, wife-beating will occur again.

2. The "victim" should never feel

guilty or blame herself for provoking the assault. No matter how your husband is provoked, he should never use physical force against you.

3. Ask your husband or your boyfriend to seek professional help. There are therapy groups and individual counsellors concentrating on this very problem.

4. If your husband loses his control, try to remain calm and avoid the confrontation. If it does erupt, defend yourself with the Defendo moves you will learn in this book. To do so, anger will have to be the strongest emotion you feel at that time, blocking out fear, shame, and confusion.

5. There are places you can go to where you will be safe. These shelters for battered wives (and their children) are listed in the telephone directory, or you can phone the government, the police, or even just the telephone operator to get the telephone number of the nearest shelter. You are not alone. The problem of battered wives is a serious and an increasing one. Seek counselling, legal action, and protection for yourself and your children — you deserve that.

Child Safety

1. A child should learn the importance of being careful, but should not develop a sense of fear. This is a fine distinction and requires patience and honest communication between all family members.

2. Make a game out of the normal rules of child safety, equating "Look both ways before crossing the street" with "Don't accept candy or rides from anyone without getting permission first," etc.

3. Warn your children repeatedly against going away with someone without telling you first. Never use the word "stranger" when warning your child, for a child cannot be expected to understand that servicemen, delivery people, the neighbor down the street, and family acquaintances should also be considered "strangers." In many cases of child assault the child knows the attacker.

4. Warn the child repeatedly, emphasizing that by going anywhere without telling you first he will worry you and make you unhappy. You should not instill fear in the child but rather a respect for your happiness and concern. As children learn from example, it is a good idea for parents to tell each other and their children where they are going and when they expect to be back, so that the children feel a part of this system of mutual respect and concern.

5. Avoid giving your child T-shirts or other garments with his name clearly printed on it. Strangers can use the name to address the child and therefore give the impression that they know the child and were sent by you to pick him up and drive him home.

6. Teach your children to cry out "Help, Daddy!" instead of "Help, Mommy!" if they are being chased or threatened. This is especially important if a grown man is chasing your child, for then bypassers will know that it isn't just the father chasing his child to punish him.

7. If your child is late and your instincts or "gut" feelings tell you that something is wrong, notify the police immediately. Rather than waste valuable time searching for the child, get professional help from the police. This is especially true if someone, even another child, tells you that your child went off with someone. Minutes can make the difference between life and death. It is definitely better to be wrong in this situation than to hesitate, and the police are always very willing to help.

8. Be sure that the child knows his full name, address, and phone number. This is essential information if the child is lost or injured. An imaginative way to help your child remember these things is to set his name, address, and phone number to a nursery rhyme or song such as Three Blind Mice, Old MacDonald, or London

Bridge. It may seem silly to adults but your child may learn more quickly that way.

9. Teach your children to use the phone in an emergency. Have important numbers by the phone, including numbers where you may be (work number, neighbor's home, and so on). At least the child should know how to dial "O" for the operator and give the necessary information.

10. Always know where your child is going and with whom. Also know how you can reach him should it be necessary.

11. Get to know your child's friends and their parents. Encourage your child to bring his friends over to the house.

12. A child should not be out at night alone and should avoid playing near empty or isolated areas. A child should not cut through alleys or vacant lots or take other short cuts home.

13. A child should not be left alone in the house. If this is unavoidable, however, he must be instructed not to let *anyone* in the house with-out your consent by phone. Many cases of child-molesting or assault involve people whom the child knows.

14. A child should be taught not to let anyone (friend, teacher, or relative included) touch or caress intimate parts of his body. If this should happen, the child should report it to his parents, a teacher, or another adult immediately.

15. The child should be taught that if anyone indecently exposes himself, he must report it to you immediately. If you are not around at the time, he should report it to his teacher, a police officer, or a trusted neighbor.

16. In cases of child abuse or incest, the child must understand that he is never to blame. This is a most difficult task, for if the child is physically abused by a parent, his inclination is to believe that it was his own fault. To help a child, one must talk openly and listen lovingly.

17. A child should be told that if he fears assault or abuse, he should run away immediately. This is hard to explain but important advice when it applies to the home environment. The child should not try to fight back but rather run away immediately to a neighbor, a relative, or a friend, or should call the Children's Aid Society's 24-hour emergency number or one of the "hot line" numbers available through the operator.

18. Obviously the burden of protecting a child from abuse or incest lies within the home environment itself. If you yourself fear hurting your child, request a neighbor or a friend to take the child for a little while when you need a break, or call your Children's Aid Society, who will be very willing to help. Also, there are various organizations, including "Parents Anonymous," and telephone hot lines where you may find help. Please do something today.

Threats against your children by other young people

19. The incidence of bullying and extortion (of money, possessions, and school lunches) in and on the way to and from school is increasing. Parents should talk to their children about crime, prejudice, and the need for mature reactions to serious situations.

20. Encourage them to confide their concerns and experiences to you. Do not get into a rage against injustice or seek "revenge" on behalf of your child. Creating a "scene" will only discourage your child from confiding in you. Ask him what he would like you to do and come up with a solution together.

21. Teenagers should realize that crimes of assault are common and unreported in their age group (and younger). They need to *think, talk, plan, and practice* for these situations with their family and friends.

22. If a teenager cannot confide in a family member, he should ask friends, teacher, a counsellor, or a local police officer for help. He is *not* the only person who faces this problem and should not try to keep it to himself. He could also try phoning a distress hot line in his area for help.

23. Students going to a known "dangerous" washroom or similar

location should go in pairs, with one acting as a "lookout" by the door and ready to go for help if necessary.

24. Parents or students should inform a school administrator about these dangerous areas. If they don't want their names known, they can explain in an anonymous note.

What Can I Do to Help Someone Else in Trouble?

1. Often a reluctance to help someone in trouble is caused by ignorance of what can be done without getting hurt oneself, or even fear of legal reprisals if one does get involved. Check with your provincial or state legislative body to see what the law says about self-defense or coming to someone's aid. In many cases you will find that you are allowed to use equal and opposite force to defend yourself or help someone else. Obviously using a shotgun to stop a purse snatcher is inappropriate overreaction.

2. If you are physically unable to help a victim far away, notify the police immediately and note down any facts that may prove helpful.

3. If the victim is in hearing range, yell to him that help is on the way. This may discourage the aggressor from remaining on the scene.

4. The question of whether to get physically involved in helping someone depends on the situation. Police officers will tell you that calls to family disputes are probably the most dangerous they receive, so don't get personally involved. Often the best course is to notify the police, let the victim know someone is coming (if possible), and be available to give the facts to the police. Use your common sense.

5. In cases of child abuse or similar situations, you can and should notify both the police and the authorities responsible for the safety of children, including the Children's Aid Society.

The "Game" of Mutual Self-Defense

1. Couples, household members, and friends should decide *in advance* on a game plan to follow if they are ever attacked or robbed. Too often people are seriously injured or killed in the confusion. It is imperative that you discuss the potential dangers and what you would do in various situations.

2. A personal code among members of a group can be both a game and a strategic plan to avoid a violent confrontation. A scratch of the nose, licking the lips, a nod of the head, lifting a foot, etc., can all signify something which only certain people will understand. If a code is used, each signal must represent a pre-planned strategy with a specific time frame. For example, if you scratch your nose, that will indicate that in ten seconds you will run toward the back door and expect everyone to follow you. Your partner must signal back with three rapid eye blinks to acknowledge your plan and approve it.

3. The "identity game" can be both useful and fun to play. Use a magazine to show the other players a picture of a person for no more than three seconds. Then have them try to describe that person *out loud*. This will help them later should they need to remember someone — describing the person to themselves aloud immediately before putting anything down on paper will reinforce their memory retention.

4. The "identity game" should concentrate first on a general description, such as sex, color, height, body build, approximate age, and clothing. Special note should be made of the pants and shoes, since shirts and coats are easily changed, while someone fleeing is less likely to change pants and shoes immediately.

5. Once you have all learned to identify basic features, practice using TV or people in the streets to identify the following details:

sex

skin color

approximate age

approximate height

approximate weight

body build

color of hair

eye color

any distinguishing scars or
physical abnormalities

speech characteristics (pitch
or accent)

exact conversation

facial hair, such as moustache
or beard

right- or left-handed

style of hair

teeth formation and color

license number (even partial),
origin of license plate (e.g.
Florida), and car make, color,
and year

type of weapon used, if any

6. When trying to note down a description of a person or a car, use whatever material is available, for example, a patch of muddy ground or a dirty car. The quicker you write something down (even on your hand), the better you will remember it later when reporting to the police.

Conclusion

Will I panic? This is probably one of the most-often-asked questions, and the answer depends on you. If a child runs in front of a car, an experienced driver, by conditioned reflex, will do what is necessary to avoid him and only then will his hands begin to sweat and shake. A mother whose child's arm is bleeding seriously applies pressure to stop it until a doctor or a paramedic takes over. Only at that point, once the crisis has been taken care of, will she feel faint.

The same is true in self-defense. People trained in Defendo who have had to use it in the past say that sometimes they don't even remember what they did, for everything

happened so fast. If you *think*, *talk*, *plan*, *and practice* for various situations, you will not be caught off guard. This doesn't take hours of practice every day for years, but it does take a conscientious effort at the beginning to think about and apply the tips in this chapter and then to learn and practice the Defendo moves shown in the following chapters. Remember to enjoy yourself and share your knowledge with family, friends, and neighbors.

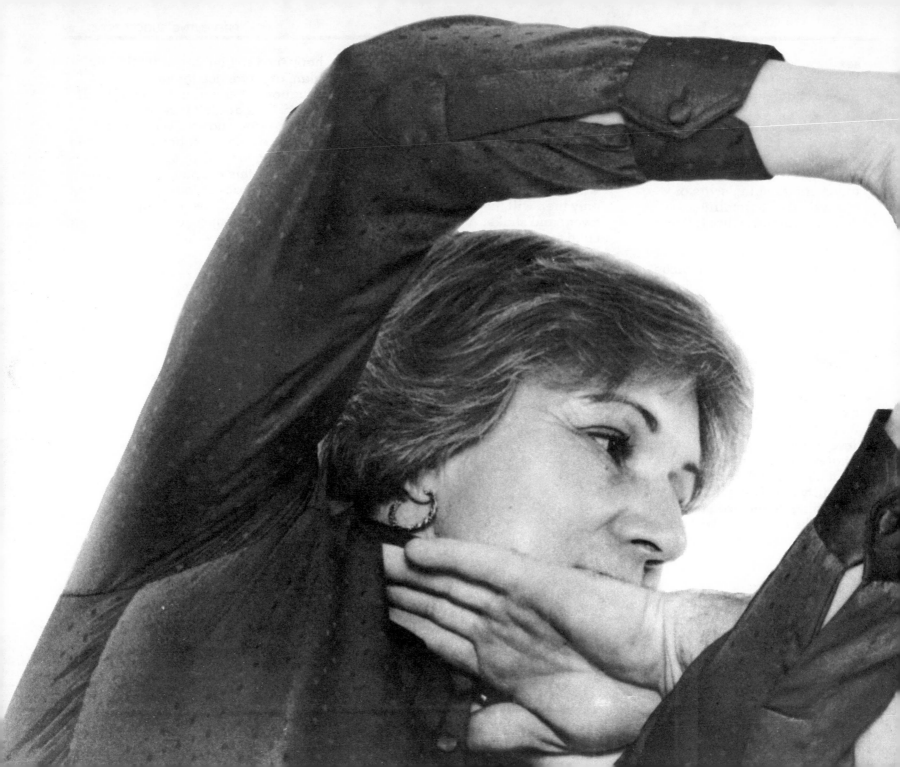

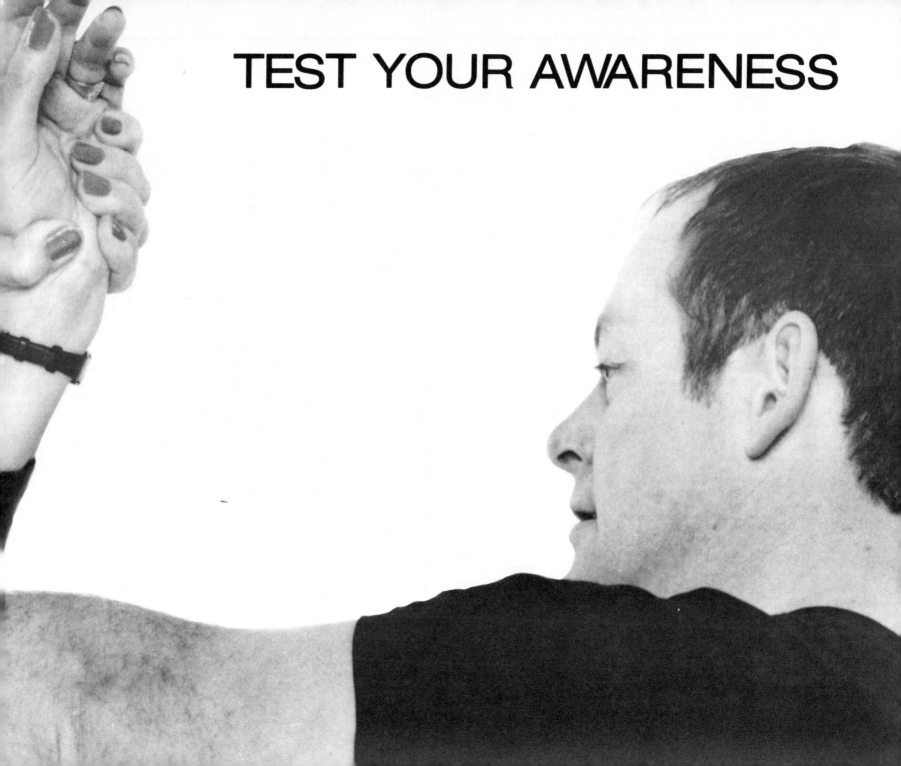

The following quiz is not a test of your intelligence but an enjoyable memory aid. It should help summarize some of the key hints offered in the *Preventive Suggestions* chapter, and you can glance back at these to find the answers if you forget them.

Try this quiz every few months, aiming for a score of 100 percent. If your score goes down, it is an indication that you should review the *Preventive Suggestions* again and begin applying more of the tips.

1. In the *Introduction* we outlined the four key elements to your personal and family safety. The first was to *think*; what are the other three? (Give 3 answers, for 6 points.)
2. When walking by yourself or with other people, what is the most important thing to remember? (3 points)
3. When walking, what should you be carrying and where or how should you be carrying it? (3 points)
4. Which side of the road or the sidewalk should you walk on? (3 points)
5. What should you do if you are asked for information on the street? (4 points)
6. What is the proper way to carry a purse or a camera case? (4 points)
7. What should you do if you feel someone is following you? (3 points)
8. What is the best way to escape from a pursuer? (3 points)
9. When should you lock your car? (4 points)
10. What should you do before getting in or out of your parked car? (3 points)
11. What should you do if your car breaks down on a highway? (Give at least 5 of 7 possible answers, for 5 points.)
12. What should you do if someone tries to get into your car? (4 points)
13. What safety precautions should you take when using public transport? (Give 5 of 8 possible answers, for 5 points.)
14. What precautions should you take if you decide to hitchhike? (Give 6 of 9 possible answers, for 6 points.)
15. What should you do if someone comes to your door unexpectedly? (Give 3 of 4 possible answers, for 6 points.)
16. What safety devices should you have on the doors and windows of your home? (3 points)
17. What should you do in response to obscene telephone calls? (3 points)
18. What should you do if you see or suspect a prowler in your home? Outside your house? (Give 5 of 7 possible answers, for 5 points.)
19. What precautions should you take before leaving your house to go on holiday? (Give 5 of 7 possible answers, for 5 points.)
20. What precautions should you take in an apartment elevator or lobby? (Give 5 of 8 possible answers, for 5 points.)
21. What two things should you do if confronted by a gunman? (4 points)
22. List the three options available to a woman threatened with rape. (This is one to think about seriously; your answers will reflect your personal decisions.) (6 points)
23. Why is it dangerous to warn your child not to go away with a "stranger"? (3 points)
24. When noting a description of someone for the police, what are the basic features you should notice first? (Give 4 of 6 possible answers, for 4 points.)

Answers

If your answer is similar to ours, give yourself full marks. Where specific points are requested, for example, 4 answers out of 7 possibilities, list as many as you remember, and give yourself points for each, up to the maximum allowed.

1. a) *Think* — about potentially dangerous situations.
   b) *Talk* — with friends, family, neighbors, and colleagues.
   c) *Plan* — as you would for a fire drill.
   d) *Practice* — to develop conditioned reflexes.

2. Be aware of your surroundings and walk assertively. Keep your head up and maintain a brisk, steady pace.

3. You should always carry your keys, so that you can quickly enter your home, place of employment, or car if necessary. Hold the key you will use next between your thumb and forefinger. A key can also be an effective weapon.

4. On a quiet street at night, walk in the middle of the road. On busier streets, walk on the sidewalk facing oncoming traffic. Walk on the curb side unless there are occupied cars along that side.

5. If a stranger approaches you requesting information or assistance, give him a short answer and walk on. If the person is in a car, stay clear of the doors, keep your answer short, and walk on.

6. The proper way to carry a purse or a camera case is to use the shoulder strap (if there is one), tuck the purse securely under your arm, and keep the side flap next to your body. Avoid carrying a purse on short trips to the store, church, or post office.

7. If you are not sure if you are being followed, turn around and look at the person, to indicate that you are aware of his presence and ready to defend yourself. Cross the street or walk over to someone else and talk with him or her until the person following you goes away.

8. If you suspect that you are being pursued, go directly to an open business or public place where people can be found, such as a hospital, fire hall, or movie theater. You could also put a parked car between you and your pursuer and scream for help. Otherwise you can run and scream to attract attention. (Kick your shoes off if they hinder your escape.)

9. You should *always* lock your car. When you leave your car unattended, locked doors discourage break-ins. When you are inside, you are protected against someone trying to enter your car at a stop light or on a secluded road.

10. Be aware of your surroundings. Check to see if there is a suspicious person lurking in an isolated area before leaving your car or walking towards it. Before getting into your car, look under and inside it carefully.

11. If your car breaks down on a highway:
    a) lift the hood;
    b) get back inside and lock the doors;
    c) put on the hazard lights;
    d) turn on the inside light at night;
    e) close all windows except for a little space to let in fresh air;
    f) wait for the police or the Motor League patrol;
    g) do not get out of your car or accept direct assistance from a motorist.

12. If someone tries to get into your car:
    a) blow your horn to attract attention or scare him away;
    b) roll your windows up tight;
    c) drive away quickly if possible;
    d) report the incident to the police at once and give as much detail as possible.

13. When using public transportation:
    a) know the schedule;
    b) be alert when waiting for the bus, subway, or train;
    c) have proper change ready;
    d) sit near the driver or the conductor, or a woman if you are a woman;
    e) in a subway or train, change cars if necessary to avoid being alone or with just a few people;
    f) hold onto purse, briefcase, or packages;
    g) if someone bothers you, go to the driver or the conductor immediately;
    h) arrange to have someone pick you up if you are unsure of your safety.

14. Avoid hitchhiking if at all possible. If you are forced to hitchhike:
    a) do not accept a ride if there is more than one man, or more than two people in the car;
    b) do not accept a ride immediately — talk to the driver for a moment first;
    c) ask the driver's destination before revealing where you want to go. Do not let the driver take you directly home;
    d) do not be afraid to refuse a ride;
    e) look to see that the doors have handles;
    f) look to see that the locks are not controlled only by the driver;
    g) do not get into the back seat if someone is already sitting there;
    h) sit in the front if you are alone with the driver;
    i) be prepared to defend yourself.

15. If someone comes to the door and you *choose* to respond to the knock:
    a) ask who is there;
    b) check through your peep-hole;
    c) ask for identification;
    d) verify the phone number of a service person or a police representative in the phone book and *then* phone the company or the police to verify the identification and purpose for calling on you.

16. All outside doors should have a one-inch deadbolt lock, as should the door of one room inside your home that you can use as a "safe room." All windows and sliding glass doors should have special locks, including small bathroom and basement windows. These should all be locked at night or when you are away, whether you live in a house or an apartment. For ventilation, windows can be opened slightly and blocked from opening further with a stick in the window rail.

17. If you receive an obscene telephone call:
    a) do not answer back;
    b) if he or she persists, notify the police and your phone company;
    c) keep a log of any persistent callers to help the police investigate.

18. If you see a prowler in your home:
    a) escape if possible (you should have a plan in advance);
    b) at night, pretend to be asleep;
    c) have a "safe room" to hide in, from which you can call the police;
    d) if you are confronted, remain calm, and cooperate as far as possible.

If you see a prowler outside:
    a) call the police immediately;
    b) turn on the outside lights, as well as a few inside lights;
    c) notify a neighbor if you see a prowler on his property.

19. When you go on vacation:
    a) have someone come by regularly to keep the grounds neat, pick up mail or papers, and check the inside of the house;
    b) use timers to turn on the lights, radio, and television in the evenings;
    c) lock all doors and windows;
    d) have a house-sitter if you are gone for a long period;
    e) contact regular delivery services to cut off delivery. Do not announce that you are going on vacation.
    f) let a neighbor or the police know when you expect to return, and where you will be in case they need to reach you;
    g) give a spare key to a friend or a neighbor in case of an emergency or a fire.

20. In elevators:
    a) stand by the controls and face other passengers;
    b) use the alarm button if you are threatened;
    c) get out of the elevator if you feel uncomfortable about another passenger;
    d) if you are going up from the lobby, do not take an elevator going down to the basement first;
    e) let other passengers push their floor buttons first; then, if you feel unsafe, push a floor higher up than the others and walk down to your floor. This will avoid revealing where you live.

    In apartment lobbies:
    a) do not let strangers in through the security system;
    b) if you find yourself in difficulty, push all of the intercom buttons or scream for assistance;
    c) do not sort or read your mail in the mail room but take it directly to your own apartment.

21. If confronted by a gunman, co-operate; do *not* play the hero. Ask him what he wants so that you can plan your own actions.

22. The choices open to a woman threatened with rape are based on your *personal* feelings and abilities. *None* is "right" or "wrong."
    a) non-resistance if you fear for your life or the lives of others;
    b) passive resistance using verbal tactics;
    c) active resistance using physical self-defense.

23. A child cannot be expected to understand that a serviceman, delivery person, neighbor down the street, or family acquaintance should also be considered a "stranger." In most cases of child assault, the child knows his molester.

24. Notice and record an assailant's:
    a) sex;
    b) skin color;
    c) hair and eye color;
    d) body build;
    e) approximate age;
    f) pants and shoes (the items least likely to be changed), and other clothing if possible.

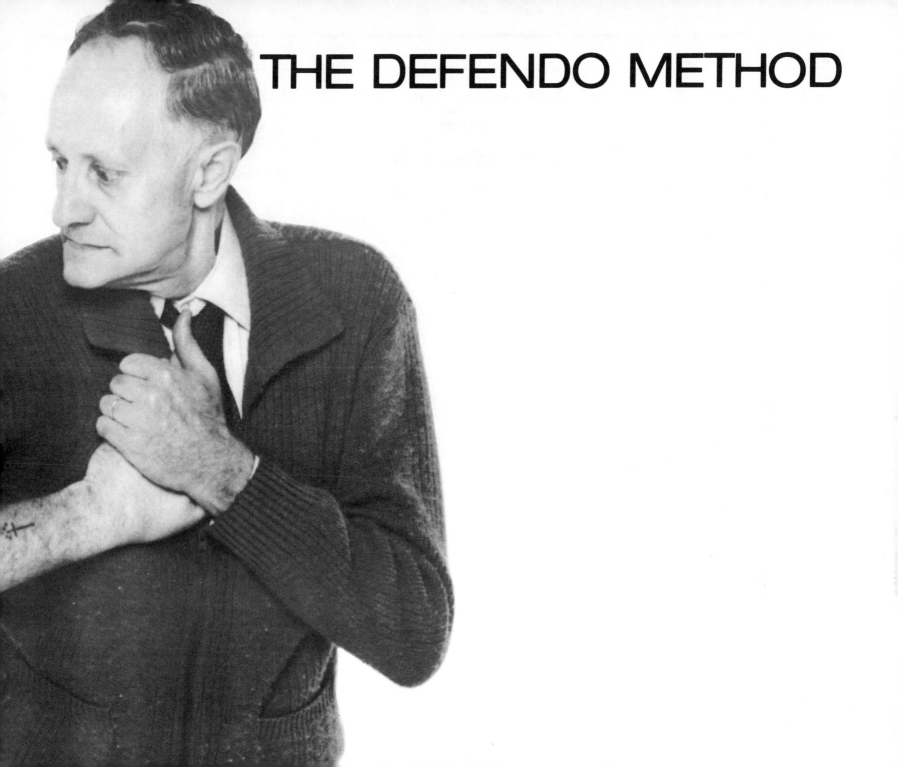

THE DEFENDO METHOD

Contents

Introduction

There may come a time when all of the preventive suggestions offered in the preceding chapter are unsuccessful, and you are forced to defend yourself against a violent attack. If that happens, you must commit yourself immediately and determinedly to doing whatever you can to protect your body. Your fear must be transformed into rage, and this only you can do. Concentrate on the inevitable natural anger deep within you. You have a right to be angry, you *must* be angry, you *are* angry. It is a matter not of "winning" but of preventing another person from hurting you. Once a violent situation has erupted, there are no gentleman's rules, and you must not hesitate to use every Defendo trick you have learned. Indecision can be very costly, so you should practice sufficiently to produce fast, strong reflex actions. Use surprise and speed to your advantage — Defendo is based on doing the unexpected.

There are several general rules to follow in a confrontation:

1. Be very observant of the opponent and your surroundings; for example, does he have accomplices? Is there an escape route? Is there someone who can help you within shouting or running distance?
2. Never underestimate an opponent, no matter what his or her sex, age, or body build. But do not lose confidence if you are much smaller. Your own strength and fitness are not of great importance when you are using Defendo techniques. Defendo is based on principles of balance, momentum, and pressure points, which are unrelated to your personal physical ability. Also, be suspicious of a boast that your opponent has a black belt in karate or judo; most professional fighters — whether martial arts experts or boxers — do not go around picking on the average citizen. Your opponent is more likely to be a beginner in one of these disciplines, trying to prove something to himself.
3. Stand squarely on both feet for firm balance, in case you are pushed or grabbed.
4. Take a few short, shallow breaths and then some deeper, slower breaths to calm yourself. This will counter the increased heart rate and irregular breathing which you will experience in a panic situation.
5. Try talking to your opponent in a calming voice. Ask him what he wants and give him any valuables he asks for. But if you are unsuccessful, try shouting aggressively, for two reasons. First, this gives the impression that you will be a serious and angry opponent. In one case an elderly woman yelled at two teenaged boys about to molest her that she'd break their ugly faces if they so much as touched her! The boys left, not quite sure what to make of her.

   Secondly, yelling as you practice or apply these moves seriously adds strength, assists your breathing, and helps to maximize your anger. As soon as the air leaves the body in a loud shout, the entire body tightens, making it less vulnerable to injury.

   The yell must come from your diaphragm rather than your throat. This technique is used by singers to project their voices more clearly and loudly, and is practiced by breathing deeply from the abdomen rather than the lungs.
6. If you are struck first and stunned, try to clinch your arms around your attacker as professional boxers often do to gain time to collect your thoughts and minimize his blows.
7. Use all of your muscles to maximize your effectiveness. Timid, unforceful blocks and kicks are not a deterrent. You may not be strong, but a surge of adrenalin will be provided by your body in a dangerous situation — *use it.*
8. An attacker who is high on drugs may feel little pain, and you will have to actually break an elbow or wrist rather than merely hurting it, in order to prevent further aggression.
9. Work on an aggressor's weak points. Notice whether he is drunk and unsteady on his feet, or clumsy with his hands, or has long hair you can pull very hard.
10. Use the aggressor's own weight and momentum against him. If he is lunging towards you as you manage to trip or pull him down to the ground, he will fall much

harder. Many of the Defendo moves utilize this principle.

11. Concentrate on accuracy. Defendo's effectiveness rests largely on the application of piercing pain to precise areas of the body. If you hit hard and accurately, your attacker will be numbed and confused. He will be diverted from his attack as he experiences pain in widely separated areas of his body. For example, you will jerk his concentration from his neck to his shin and then to his triceps, as you hit those three pressure points.

12. When you are applying pressure, do not decrease the pain level. If your assailant is caught in a painful grip, an automatic reflex makes him incapable of moving toward the center of his pain to retaliate, even if you are easily within reach. His impulse will rather be to pull away and escape, or to keep dead still if that prevents the pain from increasing. If you lessen his pain even slightly, he will experience a surge of renewed strength and will retaliate.

We do not recommend that you carry any weapon, whether it be a gun, a knife, or a spray can, since a weapon can be wrestled away and used against you. Many victims have been shot with their own guns, or have accidentally sprayed themselves because the nozzle of the aerosol can was pointed in the wrong direction or they were downwind of the spray. Moreover, weapons give a false sense of security, because most assaults occur in locations such as the victim's home, where a weapon is not carried. Concentrate on using those "weapons" that are always with you: your fingernails, fingers, hands, forearms, and elbows; your feet, knees, and legs; your teeth and skull; your voice; and the most important of all, your brain. Not only does your brain remember and apply self-defense techniques which you have learned and practiced, but it also directs the flow of adrenalin which gives you mental and physical agility far beyond your expectations.

Practice Techniques

Defendo can be practiced alone or with one or more friends. It is best to *learn* the moves with a partner first, and then to *practice* them alone or with that partner.

Practicing with others

The perfect number of people to practice with is three, as it allows two people to do the move while the third person reads out instructions and helps correct obvious mistakes. The roles are then changed so that everyone has an opportunity to practice each move.

It is necessary that your partners sincerely wish to help each other learn Defendo. Your partners must be patient and they must not resist any of your moves until you have learned to apply them well. Resistance in the learning stage only discourages people from trying to learn Defendo thoroughly. In time, increasing resistance is necessary in the practice sessions, but this should not be offered at first. Do not compete with your partner — you are not involved in a trial of strength. Even if you become excited about the new moves you have learned, refrain from demonstrating them on a friend who is skeptical about Defendo, for his ego may well cause him to resist. Defendo is based on inflicting a piercing pain on a small area of the body. You will not want to hurt a friend, so it stands to reason that the move will not work. Even experienced Defendo instructors avoid demonstrations on untrained friends, as the friends could be hurt if they resisted. Obviously, the reaction caused by Defendo in an attack situation — confusion aroused by pain in different centers of the body, and the reflex impulse to pull away from a painful grip — will not occur in a practice session, so you may be disappointed that some moves don't "work" and that your partner can easily retaliate. Remember that the speed and forcefulness of your defense in a real situation would arouse a very different reaction from your opponent.

It is very helpful for a woman to

practice with a man. This assists the woman to breach a psychological barrier against attempting to fight a man, while it helps the man realize the sincere and realistic fears of women. Also, when the man is faced with a simulated attack situation, he may realize how inadequately prepared he is to defend himself and his companion or family at the same time. He should not feel any hesitation about defending himself forcefully against a woman in a serious attack situation — gentlemen's rules do not apply.

Before starting to practice, remove all jewelry, and any sharp objects in your pockets that may hurt your partner or yourself.

Read the instructions for one entire movement right through to the end of the page before you begin to practice it, taking special note of the cautions which indicate the more painful and dangerous grips and blows. This will clarify the purpose and the end result for you, and also avoid excessive force in the more painful moves.

Begin the moves in very slow motion, and then build up speed gradually. If you are blocking punches, ask your "assailant" to aim his punches slightly harder and faster each time. If you are practicing a lengthy move, check that each component is correct before you speed up.

Apply enough pressure to receive a response from your partner and then *stop immediately*. In their exuberance at the effectiveness of Defendo, some students do the moves too vigorously.

It is up to the "assailant" against whom you are defending yourself to demand that you move slowly and without unnecessary force. When you pretend to strike a pressure point, be careful not to hit hard. The key is to *pretend* to hit hard and to yell as you do so.

The opposite problem may arise if the defending "victim" applies too little pressure in the fear of hurting his or her partner. You must be forceful enough so that in a real situation you don't defend yourself too gently. Do not just point your hand in the direction of the pressure point — actually manipulate it. Your partner must tell you if it hurts; communicate constantly as you practice so that you both benefit.

A practical solution to these problems is to tie a pillow or similar padding to your partner's arm or triceps *after* you have developed some speed and accuracy in your blocking. Then ask your partner to throw a series of three punches — for example, the straight punch at three different speeds. The first punch would be slow and light, the second punch of medium force, and the last punch a realistic blow with speed and force. Repeat the process for the other punches. This practice technique allows you to experience hitting and defending with the force necessary in a real situation.

It is vital that you practice using each of your arms or legs. Although you may be right-handed, you might have to defend yourself with your left

hand or knee. The instructions for each move follow the hand or leg used by the model in the relevant photographs. When you have practiced the entire sequence as instructed, learn and practice it all over again with the opposite hand or leg, reversing each step that mentions "left" or "right."

Vary the moves once you have learned them. "Mix and match" by trying pressure points other than the specific two or three suggested for that move, and try a variety of grips after different blocking sequences.

Do not be discouraged if the moves do not "work" immediately. Just as you had to learn to coordinate your movements when you began to swim or to drive a car, so you have to practice Defendo until your reactions are smooth and automatic.

Practicing alone

There are two ways of practicing alone. As long as you have no inhibiting audience, both methods are effective and enjoyable!

The first is a form of shadowboxing. Practice the stance, blocks, and grips in slow motion and then at normal speed, pretending that you are doing them to an opponent.

The second method is to put a bulky coat on a clothes hanger and hang it on a nail on a wall or cupboard door at a level higher than your eyes. Imagine the coat is clothing your opponent. Practice finding pressure points with your hands, elbows, feet, knees, and head. By turning your back on your "attacker" and tying the coat arms loosely around you, you can try breaking various rear bearhugs and strangles.

Practice using your left *and* right hands or legs, as you cannot be sure which you will need to use in an attack. Go through each movement using the hand or leg indicated in the instructions, and then do it again reversing left and right in each step. Begin some of the movements while you sit or lie down — attacks do not always begin with a face-to-face, standing encounter.

Remember to strike *hard* to experience the feeling of applying pressure. To practice kicking a shin or a knee, for example, you could tie a pillow or similar padding to a broom handle or a thicker piece of wood. Kick it a few times forcefully with each of your feet. This will give you an idea of the strength you must use in a real attack. However, do not attempt a move which will aggravate a troublesome back or other medical problem. There is an alternative for almost each move shown, so you do not have to master every one to be able to defend yourself effectively.

Learn the essential components of each move and concentrate on the fine points that make it effective. Speed will come only with practice. Eventually you will be able to do the moves in one quick, fluid motion, but each component must be correct first. Then you should try varying your moves and combining them in different sequences. Learn to change your plans suddenly by pretending that your assailant has altered *his* attack.

Defendo Stance

A comfortable, well-balanced stance is vital to your ability to block punches, kicks, and armed assaults. The Defendo stance is very similar to a normal standing position, with most of your weight on the back leg. From this position it is easy to move forward, backward, or sideward.

When you feel unsafe, keep your arms resting loosely in front of you, not in your pockets. Without appearing aggressive, you can raise your bent arms with palms facing forward in a gesture of "Stop. Calm down. There's no need to fight." But if a fight does erupt, your arms are already raised and you need only tighten your muscles and curl your hands into fists to be ready to block an attack.

Front view

1. Feet comfortably apart (about six inches), one slightly ahead of the other.
2. Fists at eyebrow level and facing each other.
3. Arms apart slightly wider than shoulders.
4. Keep elbows pointing down.
5. Relax — stiffen up only at moment of assault.

Side view

1. Weight on back leg for balance.
2. Fists away from your body about 1½ feet.
3. Do not lean forward.

Making a fist

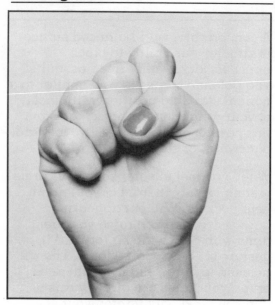

1. A strong fist is made by curling your fingers into the middle of your palm.
2. Place your thumb across your fingers.

☐ *Common Errors*
1. Do not place your thumb *inside* your fist — it may break on impact.
2. Do not let your thumb stick up from the fist — in this position it can easily snap.

Making a "knuckle fist"

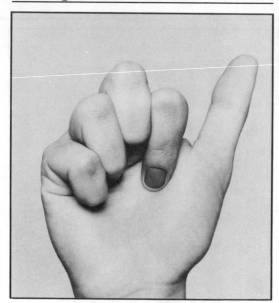

1. Sometimes it is necessary to use a knuckle to strike a pressure point. In that case, make a "knuckle fist."
2. Stretch your thumb out but curl your fingers into the *middle* of your palm, leaving the middle finger up higher than the rest.
3. Uncurl the top joint of your index finger, so that the finger extends to the base of your thumb, towards the center of your palm.

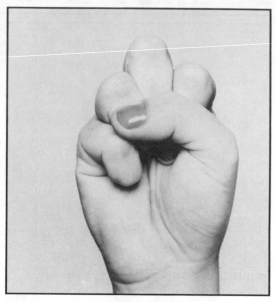

4. Cross your thumb across your fingers. This may not be comfortable but it *is* effective.

Breakfalls

If you are thrown to the ground or lose your balance in a struggle, it is important that you fall properly. The most effective "shock absorber" is a cupped hand. Practice striking a pillow and then a harder object with your cupped hand. This should make a deeper sound than if you had struck with a flat hand. The air trapped inside the "cup" acts as an absorber and lessens pain and jarring.

Many people try to break a *forward* fall by putting their hands flat on the ground in a push-up position. This is likely to cause a broken wrist or elbow. Practicing first from a kneeling position and then while standing on a mattress, cup your hands and fall, hitting the ground with your hands first at a point higher than your head. The shock will be transmitted throughout your body rather than borne solely by your wrist, elbow, or shoulder joints. Keep your head up as you fall.

A *side* fall is the most common fall. Strike the ground with your cupped hand, keeping your arm *straight* and *close to your body*. The further away from your body you strike, the more strain you will put on your shoulders. The maximum distance should be a 45° angle from your side. When you first practice this breakfall, squat down on the ground, stick one leg out straight in front of you, and then fall towards the right if you stuck out your right leg, and vice versa. Your weight lands first on your cupped hand and then moves immediately onto the *straight* forearm which is *close* to your body. Only after that point should the rest of your body touch the ground.

Breaking a fall *backwards* is more difficult because you have to thrust your cupped hands back before the rest of your body hits the ground. Keep your arms as straight as possible and hit the ground with your arms close to your sides. Roll immediately from your cupped hands onto your forearms and then onto your shoulders and back.

Pressure Points

Pressure points are highly sensitive areas of the body which you can strike, squeeze, or kick to cause sudden, piercing pain. If you can hit several of these in succession, preferably in widely separated areas of the body, your attacker will be so confused by the different pain centers that you will have time to escape. If your assailant resists a sequence of Defendo moves which you are using against him, hit or kick several pressure points before continuing with your moves.

Pressure Points and *Blocks* (see the next section) are the most important aspects of the Defendo method of self-defense. Both need to be practiced over and over again.

Front view

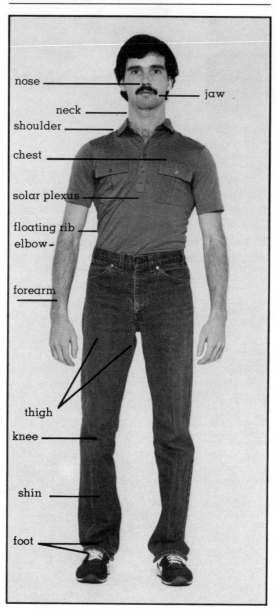

Side view

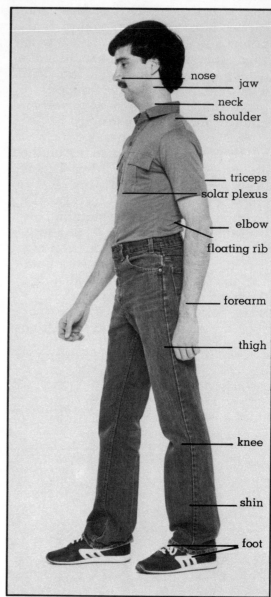

Nose pressure point

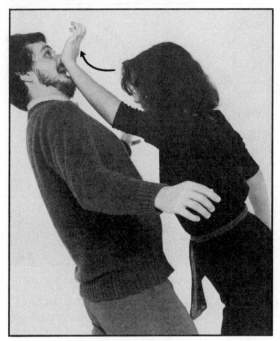

Applying force to this pressure point is extremely painful and effective. Using the heel of your palm, or either side of a straight hand, push hard *into* the skin just below the nose, and then push *up*.

This can also be applied as a striking motion. If the movement is rapid and hard, the eyes will automatically water, giving you additional time to escape.

Jaw pressure point

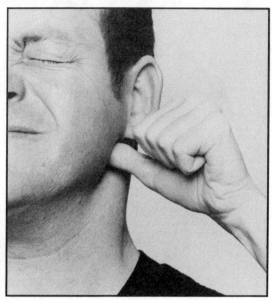

With your finger or thumb, push *inward* and then *upward* just below the curve of the jawbone, an inch or two below the ear. Pressure can be applied on one side of the head or both at the same time.

Subdue an aggressor by keeping pressure either constant or increasing. Do not decrease pressure, as the momentary relief will give your opponent a surge of renewed strength.

This move can be used to break up a fight or to lift someone out of a chair and make him walk to the nearest authority (using both hands at the same time); or it can be used when you are caught in a headlock (i.e., your head is locked in the crook of your attacker's arm) but can reach his jaw to apply pressure.

Neck pressure point

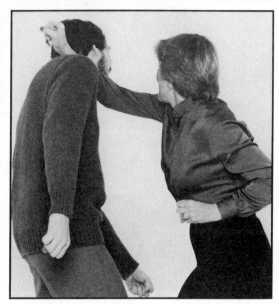

Using a swinging movement, strike the side of the neck (the right side if you are using your right arm) with the bony side of your forearm. Your forearm is a very effective weapon and is often used in Defendo. *Always hit with the bone on the same side as your little finger.*

A hard blow will cause not only pain but a momentary dizziness. This pressure point application is very effective in slowing down your attacker's reaction time. For this reason, it is used in many of the blocking movements you will learn.

Shoulder pressure point

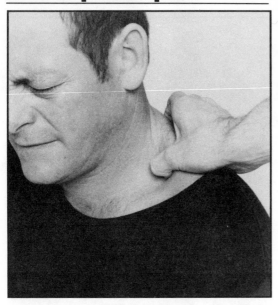

This pressure point is manipulated by using your thumb and fingers to pinch the shoulder muscle just below and in front of the neck and "roll" it forward towards your opponent's chest. Practice on your own shoulder to find the most effective spot.

Pressure can be applied from the front or the back, and is very useful in breaking up a fight by pinching both of an opponent's shoulders from behind. It will only work if your opponent is wearing a thin shirt.

Chest pressure point

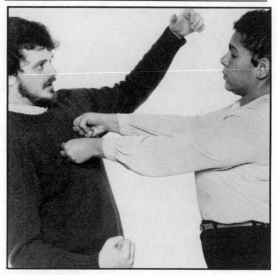

The pressure points are two spots, each a little bigger than a quarter, about two inches below the curve of your collarbone. Find them by pointing your index fingers at the sides of your neck and then drawing two straight lines downward. Probe with your fingers on your own chest, and then practice finding them immediately. This may be hard to do on yourself; ask your partner to try it on you.

Use your "knuckle fist" (both if you can) in a hard punch to these chest pressure points as your assailant charges you (for example, in a parking garage), or if you are wrestling on the ground and find yourself on top of him.

You can also use a key or your elbows to strike this area effectively, even if your assailant is wearing a thick coat. If you are grabbed in a bearhug from the front, you can use your chin to grind one of the spots.

Triceps pressure point

The triceps, the muscle at the back of your upper arm (on the opposite side from the biceps), is sensitive to pinching or striking.

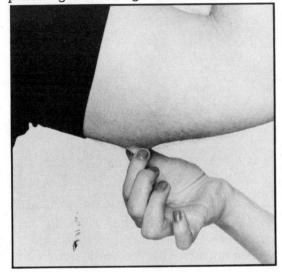

Take hold of a *small* piece of skin in that area, pinch it tightly, and then twist.

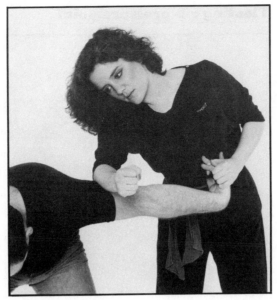

Alternatively, use your left hand to grab your opponent's left hand (from his little-finger side) with your four fingers under his palm and your thumb tucked under his little finger. Turn his hand palm up in the direction which is most awkward for him. Push his hand back so that his palm is bent towards the back of his *straight* elbow. Your partner should feel the tension in his wrist. Then slam his exposed triceps with the bony side of your right forearm (always use the bone on the same side as your little finger, and keep your fist clenched). Simultaneously pull up on his left hand with your left hand.

Now learn and practice the movement using your (and his) *right* hand.

Elbow pressure point

A blow to the back of the straightened elbow is as painful as one to the triceps, but it may, in addition, cause the joint to break. Use caution in practicing.

This move is identical to the blow against the triceps pressure point, except that you strike the back of the elbow instead of the triceps.

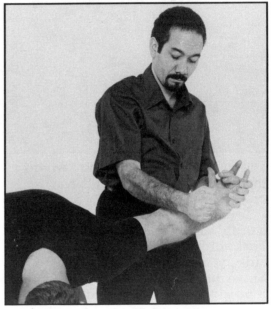

Alternatively, by pushing (rather than striking) your forearm against his elbow and pulling up on his hand, you can apply increasing and irresistible pressure to lead him to the nearest authorities.

Solar plexus pressure point

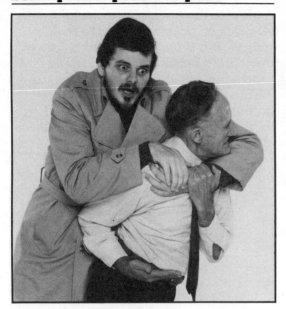

The solar plexus is that point where the ribs join the bottom of the breastbone.

To escape from a rear bearhug or a grab, shoot one of your elbows backwards and slightly upwards to strike your assailant's solar plexus. Strike quickly, and two or three times if possible. This will "wind" your attacker and give you a chance to escape.

Keep your palm open rather than in a fist while you move your elbow back, as this relaxes your muscles and thus slightly increases the distance your elbow can jerk back.

Floating rib pressure point

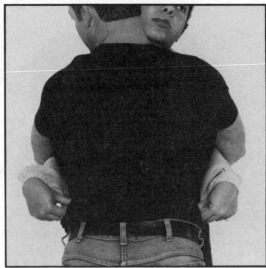

Slide your hands down the *side* of your rib cage to find the bottom, or "floating," rib. Jab your thumbs in under this rib and push upwards with your thumbnails.

You can also strike this pressure point with a fist or a knuckle to cause a sudden jolt to your attacker.

Use one or both hands.

This move is especially effective in breaking a front bearhug or a grab, or in persuading a dance partner to stop holding you so tightly!

Forearm pressure point

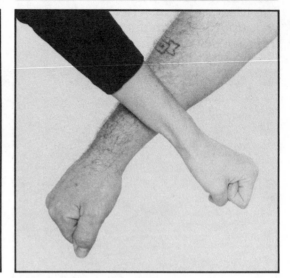

Strike the vulnerable bone of your attacker's forearm (on the same side as his thumb) with the hard, bony side of your own (the bone on the same side as your little finger).

This move is used frequently to block a punch, to knock a knife or other close-distance weapon out of an attacker's hand, or to force him to loosen a grip on you.

Thigh pressure point

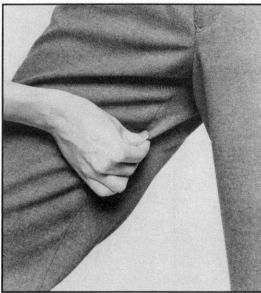

Strike the front or either side of the thigh forcefully with your knee. The pain inflicted will give you a chance to escape.

A "horse bite" is applied by pinching a *small* piece of *skin* (not muscle) from the inside of his thigh and twisting it sharply.

This pinch will break a side or a front headlock, where you are pinned down tightly but can reach his thigh.

It can also be used against a troublemaker sitting next to you at a movie, on a bus, or at a table.

Knee pressure point

Use the side of your foot to strike either side of his knee or his kneecap.

Alternatively, a hard strike with your hand, your foot, or your own knee to the *back* of your opponent's knee is likely to knock him to the ground, particularly if he is off balance.

Shin pressure point

Kick the shinbone from the front, using the inside of your foot.

You can also apply pressure to the inner *side* of the shinbone, just where the calf muscles meet the shinbone, by kicking with your toes, jabbing with your elbow, or even pinching with your fingers.

Foot pressure point

The foot is very vulnerable to pain. You can kick it on the instep or the ankle, or stamp on the toes.

High-heeled shoes are very effective for stamping, while heavy shoes or boots make a kick very painful.

If your assailant falls to the ground, stamp on the side of his ankle to delay his getting up to follow you.

These are only some of the many pressure points on the human body. The obvious ones which have not been covered here are the eyes, the throat, and the groin.

Many people find it physically repulsive to poke anyone in the eyes or hit hard at the throat area. However, in a serious situation, when other alternatives are not available, these defenses can be very effective.

The groin is not an easy area to reach for a strike. Most men have learned to protect this area automatically by bringing one leg slightly up and in front of the groin. However, an effective blow can be given if the person has been distracted by pain in another area of his body. In such a case, it is usually better to knee the groin than to kick it. Most effective at close range is to squeeze the testicles and twist them forcefully.

Blocking Punches, Thrusts, and Kicks

There are various blocking movements, depending on the angle and direction of the punch or kick you are evading.

Blocking a punch or slap aimed in a wide, circular swing at the side of your face

1. If you are practicing with a partner, the "attacker" must punch so that he would hit the side of your face if the punch was genuine. To do this, he must stand *close* to you and *aim* carefully.
2. He must alternate punching arms so that you are forced to practice using both of *your* arms.
3. You should assume the Defendo stance.
4. As the punch comes, stiffen your arms completely and move them both outward slightly.
5. If he is punching with his right hand, turn your left fist so that your forearm bone (always use the bone on the side of your smallest finger) meets his forearm pressure point. It is this contact that causes your

attacker to feel pain (and probably to drop his weapon if he is carrying one). The harder he is swinging, the more pain he will feel.

□ *Common Errors*
Your attacker is not aiming closely or accurately enough.
Your arms are not stiff enough.
Your elbows point out rather than down.
You are raising your fists above eyebrow level.

□ *Follow-up*
You should follow-up with one or more blows to pressure points, which will give you more time to escape.

6. Use your free forearm to strike the side of his neck nearest his striking arm.

7. Use the heel of your hand to strike his nose pressure point forcefully.
8. You can also kick his shin pressure point.
9. At this point, you can escape. However, if you cannot escape because you are with a child or an older person, or if you need to hold him still or lead him to the nearest authorities, use one of the *Restraints* at the end of this section.

Now learn to do the entire move with the other arm. Every move in this book must be learned and practiced both ways.

Blocking a straight punch, push, or knife thrust aimed from the front at your head

1. The partner pretending to be the "attacker" must stand close to you.
2. He must aim his punch so that it would hit your nose and follow through, pushing your head back.

☐ *Common Errors*
If he extended his arm fully, it would not hit you. He must stand closer and aim to hit and keep pushing.

3. Assume the Defendo stance.
4. As the punch comes in, step to the side with one leg.
5. In one smooth movement, swivel from the waist back towards him, with your arms in the Defendo stance. As you swivel, your stiffened arm (your right if he is punching with his left) must strike your attacker's *triceps*, or at least his elbow, with force. Continue to turn so that your striking force has more momentum.
6. Practice this movement by asking your partner to stand with his straight punching arm extended past the side of your face. Then make the swivelling movement several times, until your swivel is knocking his arm at least two feet away from you each time.

☐ *Common Errors*
Do not stop turning as soon as you hit his arm. Follow through with your swing as you would in golf or tennis.

Avoid moving any part of your upper body. Turn from the *waist* so that your arms-and-head position is stiff and does not change.

☐ *Follow-up*
At this point you can hit or kick a few pressure points and escape, or else, if you are dealing with the general public in a protective capacity, you can force your opponent to the ground by using the following moves:

1. With your left hand, slap and grab the back of his left hand (with your thumb under his wrist), and with the right hand slap the inside of that same elbow.
2. Enclose his hand in a sandwich between the thumb and the fingers of your left hand.
3. Snap his hand downwards in one quick movement so that it is pushed towards his forearm.

4. Bring his grabbed hand to your shoulder (left shoulder if it is his left hand) and continue turning his hand towards his elbow.
5. Pull his elbow to your chest.

6. In a rapid, snapping movement of his wrist, rotate his forearm at the elbow so that his hand touches the outside of his shoulder.
7. Draw the back of his wrist down the center of your chest, keeping the elbow stationary.
8. Stand *erect*.
9. The pain should be felt in his wrist only, and should cause him to fall down on his back.

□ *Common Error*
Do not use your whole body to force against the wrist. This actually takes some of his pain away. Use your *hand* to exert the snapping pressure.

10. Maintain your grip until your opponent is flat on the ground.
11. Escape at this point, or apply a restraint (see *Restraints*) if you need to hold him still.

Blocking a punch or knife thrust to the ribs or stomach

This block can be used to block a quick punch to the lower ribs or stomach, or it can be used in a knife attack. Often an experienced fighter will stand calmly in front of you with his knife held across his thigh. Without warning he will bring the knife upward in an attempt to stab you in the stomach or chest.

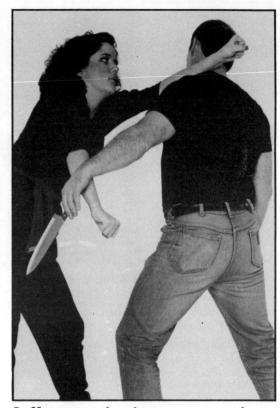

1. The "attacker" must aim his punching hand from the level of his thigh towards your lower ribs or stomach.
2. He must stand very close to you.

□ *Common Error*
The punch would miss you altogether as the "attacker" is too far away.

3. From your Defendo stance, snap your arm (right arm if he is thrusting with his left hand) down across the middle of your body, and *close* to your body, as you take a step out of the way. Your forearm bone should make contact with his forearm pressure point.
4. Follow through on your block until your arm is fully extended and about waist-high.

□ *Common Error*
The block is less effective if you bring your arm down about a foot away from your body, anticipating the punch. Snap it down close to your body and follow through.

5. Use your other forearm to smash the left side of your attacker's neck.

☐ *Follow-up*

At this point you can escape. However, if further action is necessary, there is an appropriate follow-up.

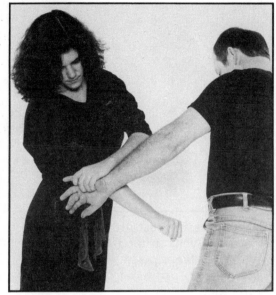

1. Slide your hand (left hand if he is using his left hand) down your assailant's arm and pick up his little finger and palm in a firm grip.

2. Make a large arc by swinging his arm in a loop up over your head to the *other* side of your body.
3. Keep his arm in a straight line with his two shoulders, not behind or in front of them.

4. Once you have his arm stretched in front of you, keep his elbow straight and his fingers pointing straight up.
5. Step close to him.
6. Use your forearm bone to strike or push down on the triceps or back of the elbow, to force him to the ground.
7. Simultaneously pull his hand up. The combined movement will cause severe pain.
8. Remember to stand on or kick far away any weapon that you have knocked to the ground. If you run away, take it with you unless it hinders your escape in any way.

Blocking a snap-kick

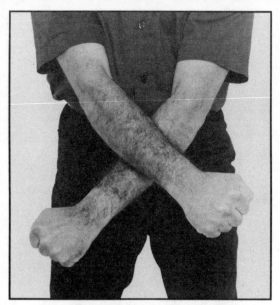

1. Your attacker must stand close to you.
2. He must snap his kick from his knee and aim his foot at your groin. This is a very rapid kick.

3. From your Defendo stance, move your arms downward (close to your body) to cross at about mid-forearm.
4. Lay one arm flat on top of the other in an "X" and stiffen them.
5. Keep your fists tight to avoid breaking a finger.

☐ *Common Errors*
One or both arms are turned sideways instead of being flat against each other.

The arms are not held solidly and tightly against each other.

The "X" is too small or too large.

6. Hit his rising leg with the bony cross of your arms at about his shin pressure point.
7. Move your groin out of the way of his foot.
8. Keep your eyes on your opponent in case he is about to punch you at the same time.

☐ *Follow-up*

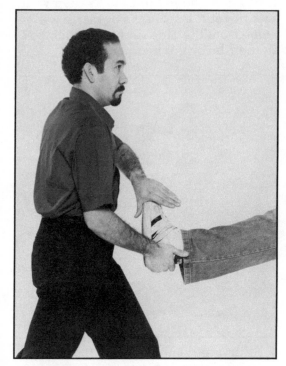

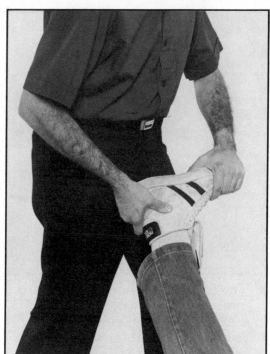

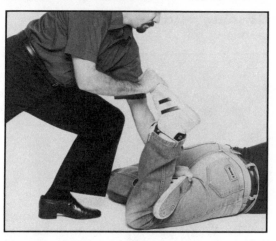

9. Keeping your forearms crossed, quickly open your hands and grab the ankle of the leg you have just hit. Simply throw your attacker off balance by raising his leg. He will fall on his back. (If you lift his leg too violently, he could land on his neck and break it.) You can escape at this point.

10. If restraint is necessary, place your hand on your opponent's heel (your right hand if it is his right heel) and grab his toes with your left hand. Tuck your elbows in.

11. If you are holding his right foot, snap the toe end to the left. This must be a rapid, sharp movement of the *toe end only*, not a general twisting of the entire leg, or even of the whole foot. If the movement is rapid enough, he will have to flip over onto his stomach. Stand erect and use only your arm to effect the snap, not your whole body.

12. Tuck his left leg across the back of the knee of the right leg (which you are still holding).

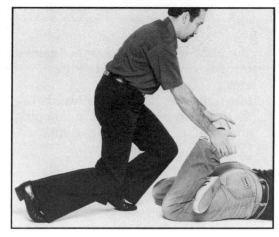

13. Bend the right leg at the knee to enclose the left leg tightly.

14. Kneel on the left shinbone to increase pressure. This is extremely painful, so use caution in practice.

15. Push the toes of his right foot towards his head and keep pressure constant or increasing.

Evading a kick while on the ground

1. If you have fallen to the ground on your back and your opponent comes towards you, get ready to kick back.
2. If he circles you, use your hands to pivot around on your bottom, keeping your feet pointed directly at him.

3. If he comes close enough, give him a very hard, sideward kick to his shin or knee using either side of your foot. If possible, hook one foot behind his ankle and pull, just as you kick him with your other foot. This will increase the pain *and* cause him to fall backwards.

□ *Alternative*
If you don't have the time to keep your feet in your assailant's path, he will come from the side and try to kick you in the ribs or the head.

1. With great speed, roll *into* his kick, taking most of his momentum away. As he will have expected you to roll away, the element of surprise will also be in your favor.

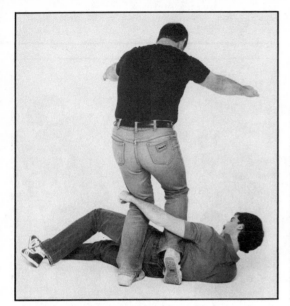

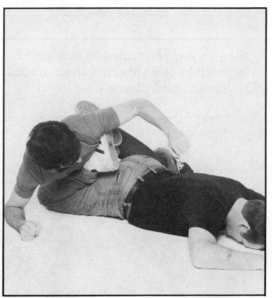

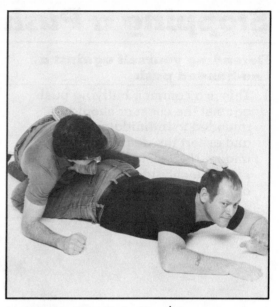

2. With a free forearm, strike forcefully against the back of his knees, which will knock him to the ground.

3. To inflict additional pain before you escape, or to restrain him, roll against the shins of his bent legs after he has fallen over you.

4. Grab a handful of hair from the front of his head and pull it backwards.

Stopping a Push

Defending yourself against a two-handed push

1. This is a common bullying push against the chest or shoulders, intended to intimidate the victim and assert the aggressor's "tough" image. No resistance is expected. First you should try to talk your way out of this situation.

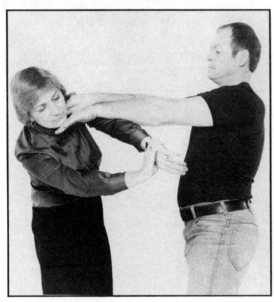

2. If you are unsuccessful, link your hands in front of your thighs and then swing your arms in a wide arc high up to one side and then across in front of and above your head.

3. Keep your body and arms moving in the same direction and follow through. Your momentum will have knocked his hands away and twisted his body away from you.

4. Catch hold of his nearest hand and stretch his arm in front of you to expose his triceps and elbow, so that you are ready to strike those pressure points if the situation warrants it. You can also kick the back of his knees.

Defending yourself against a one-handed chest push or shirt grab

3. Raise your other arm in the Defendo stance and maintain good balance.

1. First try to talk your way out of this attempt to intimidate you.
2. If you are unsuccessful, *slap* and hold his hand against your body with one of your hands. Use your left hand if he is pushing with his left hand. Grab his little finger for added restraint and control.

4. Turn from the *waist* to your left if he is using his left hand, to your right if he is using his right hand. This will expose his triceps.
5. With your free arm, use your forearm bone to smash or push against the back (not the top) of his straightened elbow or his triceps. The amount of force you decide to use should depend on his aggressiveness and the circumstances.

Grips

These are used to immobilize an opponent, to force him to the ground, or to escort him elsewhere. When practiced thoroughly, they can cause acute pain to your opponent. There are three Hand Grips and four Finger Grips. Try them from sitting, lying, and standing positions.

HAND GRIPS

Palm grip

This grip can be used after you have blocked a straight punch or a chest grab, or at any time when you are able to get hold of your attacker's hand.

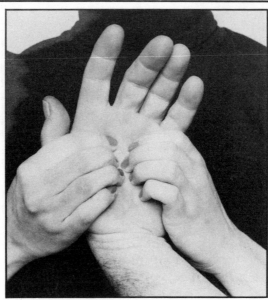

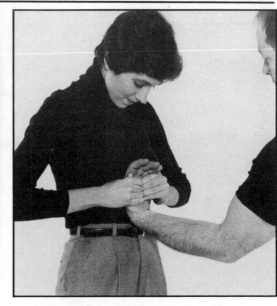

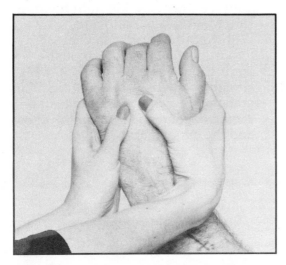

1. Pick up his hand so that his palm faces himself.
2. Place both of your thumbs on the back of his hand, about half an inch below his knuckles to prevent slippage.

3. Grip his palm with all eight of your fingers. Your fingers must not extend past the palm to the wrist.

4. If you can, bring his hand to your solar plexus for added strength, keeping your elbows tucked in. However, this move can also be done away from your body.

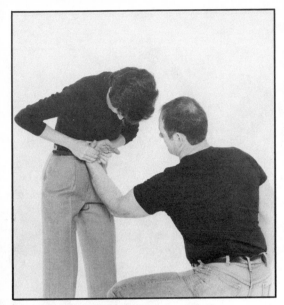

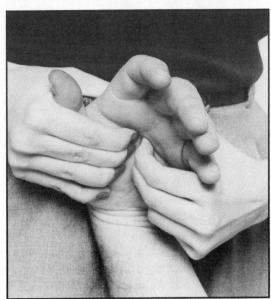

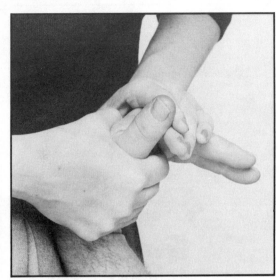

5. This is a critical point. With a *sudden*, *snapping* movement (not a push), bend his palm forward and down, while simultaneously you bend at the waist. Your hands should rest against your body for leverage. Tuck your bottom out of the way as his elbow may hit your groin.

□ *Common Error*
You are pushing or rolling your opponent's hand instead of snapping it quickly. A push or roll is resistible; a snap is a piercing pain which is almost impossible to resist.

6. The snapping movement will bring your opponent to his knees. To put him on his back, lift his hand very slightly and then *snap* it to the right if it is his left hand, to the left if it is his right. He will fall onto his back quickly, and his feet could easily hit you. Be careful. Hit a few pressure points, such as his ankle, and escape.

1. You may find it easier to grip his hand with only one of your hands, but in the same way.
2. Bring it to your body and bend the palm downwards.
3. Then use your free hand to smash down on his bent fingers across the knuckles and keep pushing down.

Sandwich grip

This grip is used against a hand coming over your shoulder or under your arm from the back. You would use it to take your attacker to the ground immediately after breaking a rear bearhug, a strangle, or a hair grab.

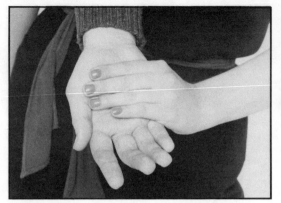

1. Grab and turn the person's palm up to bar his arm.
2. Lay the fingers of your left hand (if you are holding his right hand) *flat* across his palm. (However, this grip works just as well if your opponent is making a fist.)
3. Keep your thumb at the back of his hand.
4. Do not cover his wrist.

5. Repeat this movement with your other hand, thus sandwiching your opponent's four fingers *and* thumb between your hands (which are one on top of the other). Keep your fingers *flat*.

6. Twist his hand to the right if it is his right hand, and roll his arm off your shoulder.
7. Stand still and erect, since leaning with your shoulders will only relieve the piercing pain he should feel in his wrist.
8. As you roll his arm, keep his elbow straight so that his body begins to fall in a wide, circular arc.
9. As you complete the roll, bring his hand to touch your right hip. This puts pressure on his wrist rather than twisting his whole arm.
10. At this point he will fall to the ground.

Fist grab

You can use this grip if your opponent threatens you with clenched hands, or grabs your hair or shirt from the front in his fist.

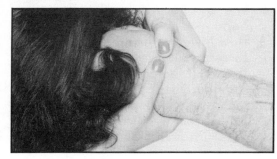

1. Lean your head forward to give you easier access to your opponent's hand.
2. Grab his clenched fist with your *thumbs on top* and your fingers underneath. This is uncomfortable but effective.
3. Squeeze as hard as you can, allowing *no space* between his hand and your fingers. (Ask your partner to try and twist his hand away. If he succeeds, you should be squeezing tighter; it should hurt his wrist to twist out.)

4. If your attacker is pulling your hair with his left hand, turn quickly to your left, and vice versa. If you turn the wrong way, into his chest, you may end up in a rear strangle.
5. Make only a half-circle, so that you have your back to him. Do not turn around completely.
6. Just before you make your quick turn, kick his shin to loosen his grip on your hair or your shirt.
7. As you turn, raise his arm over your head.
8. Stand solidly for good balance.

9. When you have stopped turning, continue to turn his extended arm and bring his hand down to your left hip, if you are holding his left hand. It must touch your hip.
10. This causes a piercing pain in his wrist which will force him to the ground. You have to be holding tightly *throughout* the move.
11. Hit two or three pressure points and escape.

FINGER GRIPS

Thumb grip

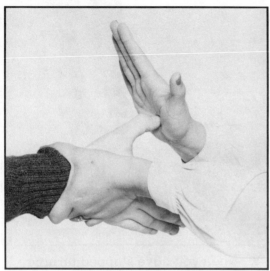

1. With your left hand, hold your opponent's right wrist.
2. With your right hand, bury the tip of his right thumb in the inner edge of the cushion below your thumb, a little lower than and to the right of the center of your palm.
3. Push up and against his knuckle.
4. Keep your own fingers pointing straight up.

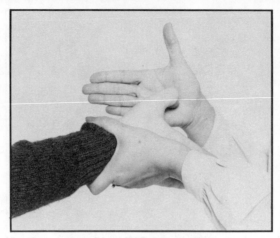

5. Turn your hand 90 degrees, keeping your fingers straight.

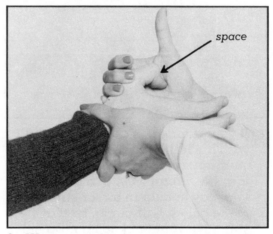

space

6. Wrap your fingers around the ball of his thumb.
7. Make sure you do not bury or cover the joint at the middle of his thumb. There must be a *space* between his joint and your palm.

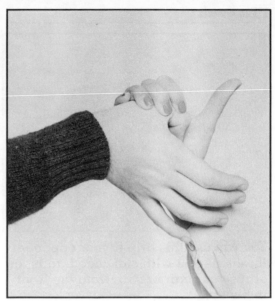

8. Let go of his wrist with your left hand.
9. Now *lower* your right wrist to increase the pressure on his thumb. If the hold is correctly applied, your opponent should be on his toes with pain.
10. At this point you can hit a few pressure points and escape.

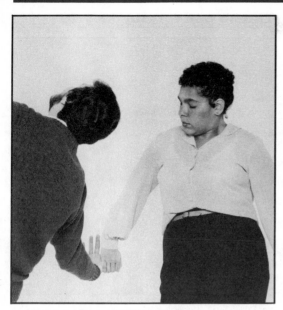

One-finger grip

In a body grab it is easy to pry a finger loose by pushing against the tip of the fingernail.

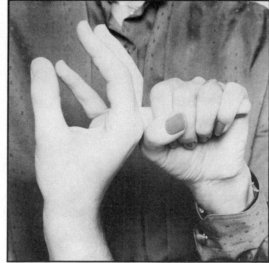

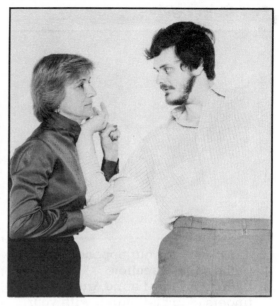

11. However, if you want him to fall to the ground, step back, letting go of his wrist, and bring his hand across your right side, towards your right hip. If this is done with one quick, flowing movement, he will fall down on his back.
12. Then escape, or restrain him with one of the *Restraints* at the end of this section.

1. Grab hold of one of the fingers of your opponent's right hand with your left hand, so that your thumb is at the back of the base of his finger, with the back of your hand facing in the same direction as his open palm.
2. Squeeze tightly and pull back on his finger in the direction of his forearm.

3. As you pull your opponent's finger back, his instinct will tell him to lift his elbow to relieve pressure. To prevent this, hold his elbow still with your other hand, keeping his forearm vertical. Use caution while practicing.
4. Rest his forearm against your chest if you need extra support.
5. From this position, you can escort him to the authorities, or else force him to the ground and escape. He should be on his toes or knees with pain.

Two-finger grip

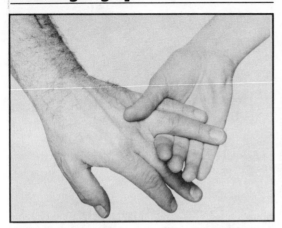

1. Stand next to your opponent, facing in the same direction.
2. Using your right hand, grab the last fingers of his left hand, with your palm up and his palm down.
3. Pull his fingers back and up slightly so that he cannot bend them.
   Use caution while practicing from this point.

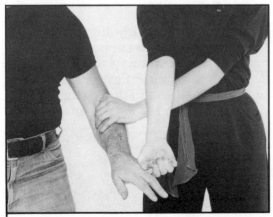

4. Move your free hand underneath your own right arm, and grab the inside elbow joint of your opponent's trapped arm.

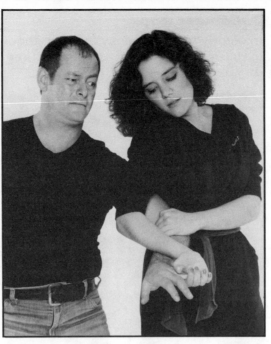

5. Using caution in practice, as this is very painful, pull his elbow across your chest as you extend your own elbow across his. This is called a cross-over.
6. Pull his fingers upwards to prevent him from bending his wrist. Exert more pressure by pulling the two fingers which you are gripping sideways away from his other fingers.

Thumb and forefinger grip

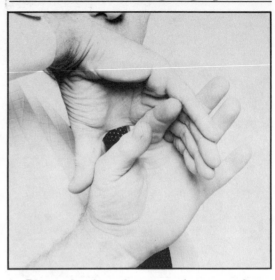

1. Place the four fingers of your right hand across the index finger of his left hand.

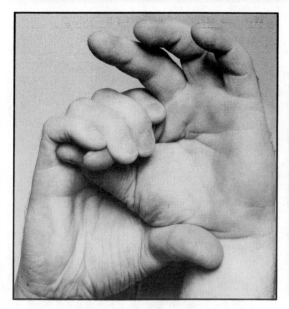

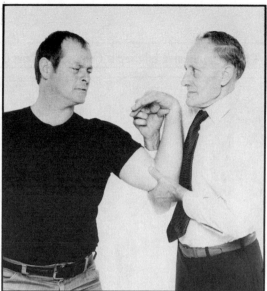

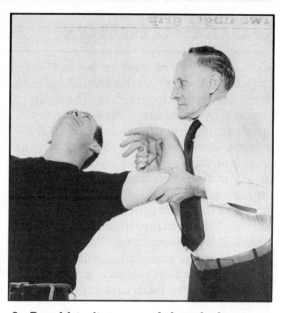

2. While pushing his index finger downward towards his palm, slip your thumb completely below the ball of his thumb at his wrist. *Do not allow your thumb to move from his wrist*, even though this may be uncomfortable. No matter how small your hand is, the movement is very effective.

3. As his index finger meets his thumb, keep pushing them both down towards the inside of his forearm.

4. Bring his hand to a position where his elbow will be down and his forearm pointing straight up.

5. Anchor his elbow with your free hand.

6. Bend his finger and thumb down suddenly towards the wrist to increase pain in the wrist, and keep the elbow almost stationary. The piercing pain in his wrist should make your opponent fall on his back.

7. Strike two or three pressure points and escape.

Come-alongs

Come-alongs are used to "escort" an opponent or even just a friendly drunk from one place to another. The pain caused by pressure if they resist will discourage them from doing so. Of course, it is necessary to distract your opponent with a strike to a pressure point or even just with talk before applying a come-along.

There are different come-alongs to be used in a variety of situations, with varying degrees of pain. In most come-alongs, your opponent should be on his toes while you are escorting him, due to the pain and pressure exerted.

The "pinned biceps" come-along

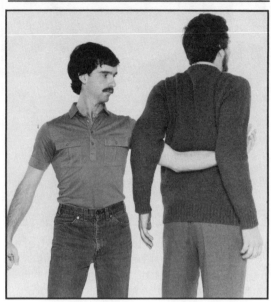

1. Move behind and slightly to the side of your opponent, facing in the opposite direction.
2. Put your arm which is nearest to him between his nearest arm and his side, and then continue to "thread" your arm behind his back.

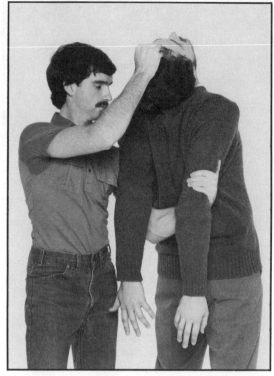

3. Hook your hand all the way around the biceps of his far arm, as high up as possible, thus pulling his arms together firmly. This will exert pressure on his back.
4. Reach over his head with your free hand and grab the front of his hair. Pull it backwards. (If he is bald, you can grab his nostrils.) This movement will force him to look upwards, disorienting him.
5. If he keeps trying to break free, or if you cannot reach his hair, collapse his knees from the back.
6. Escort him where you wish.

The wrist lock

This is very effective in a sitting position — for example, in a theater or on a bus. If you wish to practice in this position, have your partner put his hand on your knee, then slip your hand underneath his forearm and apply the wrist lock.

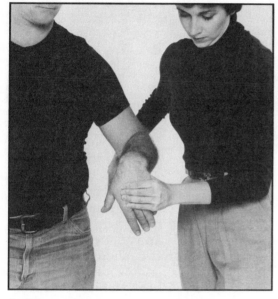

1. Move close to your opponent.
2. If he is sitting or standing on your right, grab his left hand with your left hand, placing your fingers across the back of his hand and your thumb under his wrist.
3. Roll his hand down so that his fingers point straight down.

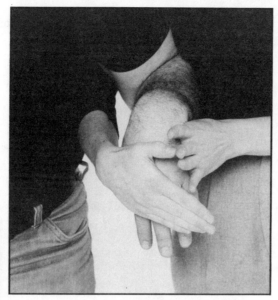

4. Move your right arm all the way around the back of the elbow of his trapped arm, tucking his elbow tightly under your arm. This will prevent his elbow from escaping. (If you are restraining a smaller person, you may not be able to keep his elbow under your arm, but you can still tuck it against your side for firm support.)
5. Place your right hand over his trapped hand so that the *bottom of your palm* covers *his index finger knuckle.*
6. Remove your left hand as you place the rest of your right hand across his knuckles.

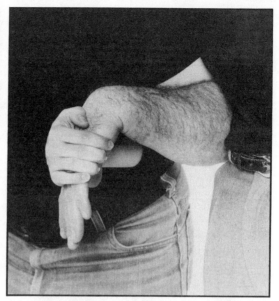

7. Shift the fingertips of your right hand under the base joint of his little finger and pull it up towards your own palm.
8. While you pull up on the little finger, also push his entire hand back, towards his elbow joint.
9. Make sure that your thumbs are on the top, not the inside, of his wrist.
10. Keep his forearm parallel to the ground.
11. You can replace your left hand on top of your right hand for added strength, if you prefer.

The "barred-arm" come-along

This move is especially useful for security guards or personnel who have to escort troublemakers. Your opponent can be standing, sitting, or lying down when you use it.

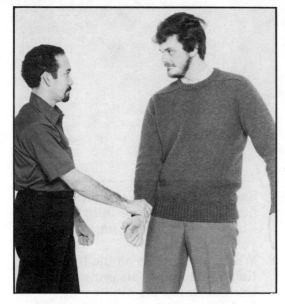

1. Stand close to your opponent and grab his right wrist with your right hand.
2. Turn his wrist so that his palm faces up.

3. If your opponent is taller than you, bring him down to your level by collapsing the back of his knees with your own knee.
4. Stretch your left arm across the front of his throat. Strike lightly if necessary.

5. Then bend your left arm to circle his barred arm high up near his shoulder. Wrap your arm around his. Your forearm should be under his triceps or elbow, and your hand should be either touching your right shoulder or gripping your right biceps for support.
6. Stand *erect* and pull down on his wrist so that pressure is exerted on his triceps.
7. Stretch his arm away from you as you pull down, to increase discomfort.

☐ *Common Errors*
1. You must stand *erect* to cause pain.
2. You must actually touch your opposite shoulder or grab your opposite biceps.

The "hair-grab" come-along

This is a very effective method of grabbing your opponent's hair which will enable you to escort him to the authorities, or assist you to restrain him.

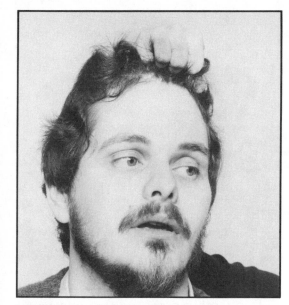

To disorient or unbalance your opponent:
1. Stand behind him.
2. Reach over the top of his head and pull the hairs at the front of his head *backwards*.

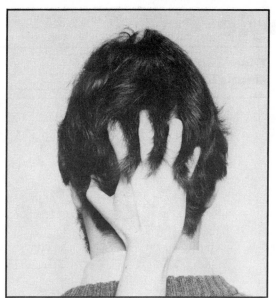

To escort your opponent forward:
1. Stand behind him.
2. Slide your open hand up his head, starting at the base of his skull at the top of his neck.

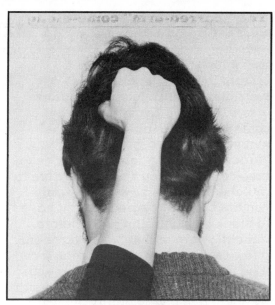

3. When your entire hand is in contact with hair, make a tight fist to catch the hairs in it, and push *upwards*. This is more painful and effective than pulling downwards.

Escaping a Strangle

Strangles are applied to stop a scream, intimidate, eliminate resistance, or kill. Many stranglers also get a "high" from seeing the control they have and the fear their victims express.

Your immediate defence must be to break his hold. You will not be able to inflict pain or overpower him while you are being strangled, so you have to break his controlling grip before inflicting pain or injury. You have only a few seconds in which to break loose if he is serious about strangling you.

In practice, your partner should start by holding you very lightly. As you perfect the move, the pressure should become stronger and stronger, so that you will not panic in a real-life situation. However, too much pressure could cause you to black out, or feel uncomfortable for a day or two.

Escaping a two-handed strangle from the rear

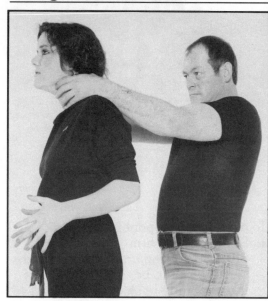

This escape is very similar to the one from a front strangle.

1. Bring either arm straight up from your shoulder and keep it straight and behind your head so that you cannot see your fist.

2. Turn forcefully *towards* the arm you have raised.
3. Move and step on to the same foot as the arm you have raised, for balance.
4. The pressure against his fingers will break his hold.

5. Follow through with your turn, which will probably tuck his arms under your raised arm.
6. Only at this point should you bring your arm down quickly to wrap it around *his* arms, catching them in the crook of your elbow.
7. If this is done quickly and forcefully, you will hurt and possibly break the straightened elbow.

8. In order to turn, you had to step on to the same leg as the arm you had raised (see step 3). Now use the free leg to knee your assailant in the thigh or the groin.
9. Use your free hand to hit his nose pressure point, which will probably knock him to the ground. Escape.

Escaping a forearm strangle from the rear

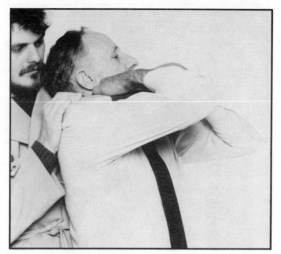

This escape is used when your throat is caught from behind by your assailant's forearm. As this strangle is from the rear, it is usually a surprise and you will have to react automatically — there is no time to think.

1. Your prime concern is to loosen the tension on your throat to allow you to breathe.
2. Use both hands to grab his lower forearm, with your thumbs *and* fingers on top of his forearm.
3. Lift both of your elbows up.
4. *Snap* your elbows down again, tucking your chin into the small space you have created with the sharp snap downwards.
5. There will be pressure against your chin, but you will be able to breathe.
6. As soon as you have tucked your chin in, turn your chin into the hollow of your assailant's elbow joint. This gives you more space.
7. Lift one leg and *lightly* find his leg or foot.
8. *Only then*, strike *hard* against his foot or the front of his shin.

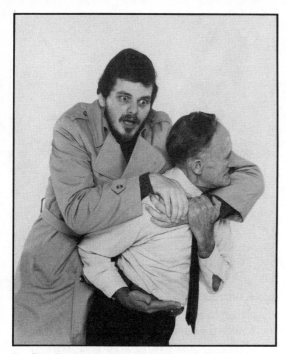

10. Jab him two or three times in quick succession.
11. Turn around quickly to the left as he releases you.
12. Grab hold of his left wrist with your right hand.
13. Maintain firm balance.
14. Strike forcefully at his nose pressure point with the heel of the palm of your free hand.
15. Hit other pressure points (the thigh, the shin) if necessary, and escape.

□ *Alternatives*
a) In close quarters where you are not able to move your foot or bend your elbow, secure breathing space and then use your right hand to squeeze his testicles and twist them hard.
b) You may also need to move your hand up and back to jab hard at his eyes.
c) After you have broken the stranglehold and secured his hand, you may prefer to apply the Sandwich Grip (see *Grips*) and roll him off your shoulder onto the ground. This eliminates the need to turn, if balance is difficult for you.

9. At about the same time, jab him in his solar plexus with your elbow. Use your right elbow if he is strangling you with his left forearm. Keep your palm open rather than in a fist, as this slightly increases the distance your elbow can move back.

Escaping a strangle from the front

1. This escape can be used if you are being strangled with either one or both of his hands.

2. If he is using two hands to strangle you, bring either of your arms straight up from your shoulder. Keep it straight and behind your head and behind your line of vision so that you can't see your hand. If he is using one hand to strangle and the other to hit you, block the slap as you normally would, using your right forearm if he is punching with his left hand, and raise your other arm.

3. Clench your fist.

4. From your waist, turn your *upper body* forcefully against his hands in the direction away from your raised arm. Keep your arm perfectly straight above your head. Your shoulder will make contact with his fingers, and the sudden turn will slide his fingers off your neck.

5. Keep your feet still and maintain firm balance as you swivel.

6. *After* the hold is broken, turn back towards him. Drop your arm down quickly and then *raise* it again forcefully so that your bony forearm smashes the side of his neck or face. Use caution in practice as smashing accidentally against your partner's throat is very dangerous.

☐ *Common Error*

You do not need to bring your arm down across your opponent's arms to break his hold. In fact, this will lessen the pressure the correct move exerts. The intention is to work against his fingers, not his strong forearms.

Escaping a short-arm strangle from the front

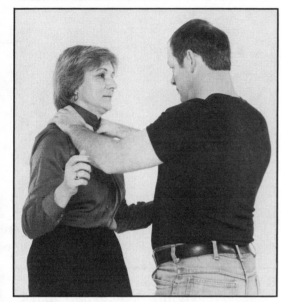

This escape is used when the strangler is standing very close in front of you and you can reach his throat. It is the best escape to use when you have been pushed into a corner so that you have no room to lift an arm behind you. This is a very painful and dangerous defense, so use extreme caution in practice.

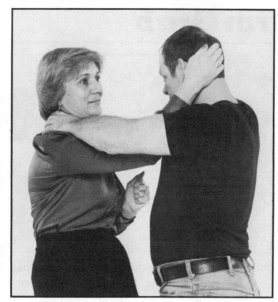

1. Bring one hand up between your opponent's arms and place it at the back of his head, on the ball of his skull. Lean your forearm against his chest for leverage.

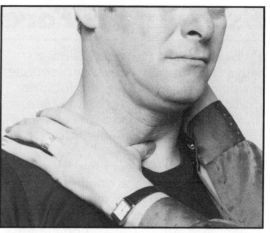

2. Bring your other hand up between his arms and jab your thumb forcefully into his windpipe. Use caution in practice, as even slight pressure is painful.
3. As you jab, pull his head forward into your thumb with your other hand.

□ *Alternative*
Even if it is not possible to place your hand at the back of his head, you can still jab a thumb into his throat. You may need to use your other arm to block a blow if he is strangling you with one hand and slapping with the other.

Escaping a Forearm Grab

Probably two of the most common ways of beginning an assault against a woman are strangles and forearm grabs. Both are easy to break. Men should also learn to escape, as these are common in two-men-against-one-man attacks.

The purpose of most forearm grabs is to pull the victim to another location. The aggressor always assumes you will resist by pulling in the opposite direction. Fortunately, you do not have to match his strength and momentum. First you surprise him and relieve pressure by stepping closer to him, and then you work against his weakest point in that position — his thumbs.

Escaping a two-handed grab

1. This grab shows your forearm caught between your attacker's hands, with his thumbs on *top* of your arm.

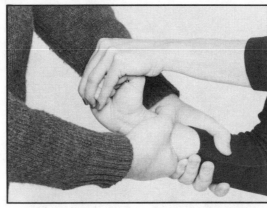

2. Make a fist with your grabbed hand.
3. Suddenly step in the same direction as his pull, except do it quicker than he is moving. Step right into him, stamping hard on his foot if possible.
4. As you do so, bring your free hand in over the *top* of his arms to secure a strong hold on your own fist.

5. Drop your captured elbow suddenly until it *touches* his body.

6. Immediately use your covering hand and entire body to pull your wrist forcefully back towards yourself.
7. Because you are using your straight forearm as leverage, your attacker will be forced to loosen his grip. If he was pulling you hard when you stepped into him, you will probably be four to six feet away from him when you release yourself. (Be careful not to hit your own nose with your released fist!)

☐ *Alternative*
If the attacker grabs you with his thumbs *underneath* your forearm, bring your free hand in (to grab your own fist) *underneath* his arms. Move in close while you take hold of your fist. Then pull *down* against his thumbs and towards yourself.

Escaping an opposite-hand grab

This forearm grab — your attacker's left hand gripping your right forearm, or vice versa — is probably the most common. Whether your attacker's thumbs are facing forward or backward, the escape is the same. However, when the thumb is facing backwards, it will take the entire escape move to break his hold. When the thumb is facing forward, you will be free after doing only half of the move.

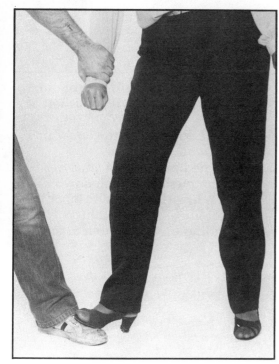

1. The attacker is gripping your forearm with his left hand and probably pulling you with him.
2. Step in right up to him, stamping hard on his foot.

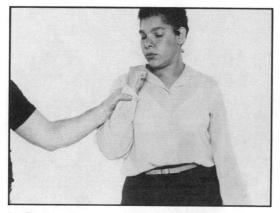

3. Bring your grabbed arm in a circular motion closely across your chest to touch its own shoulder immediately. This may take some effort while you are practicing, but in a real situation you will have surprise on your side because he will be expecting you to pull away in the other direction.

4. From your shoulder, drive your arm straight up.

□ *Common Error*
Often people will try to do this step without first bringing arm to shoulder. Your attacker will not be able to resist you if you bring your arm to your shoulder and then shoot straight up, but he can resist if you try to drive the arm straight up as soon as he grabs you.

5. If you are not already free, forcefully swing your arm *forward* in a circle.
6. With your arm straight, keep swinging it until the force works against your attacker's thumb to break his grip.
7. Kick the side of his knee and hit any other pressure point, and escape.

□ *Common Error*
If you swing backwards, you can be resisted. Try it both ways to prove this and then never practice backwards again.

Escaping a same-hand grab

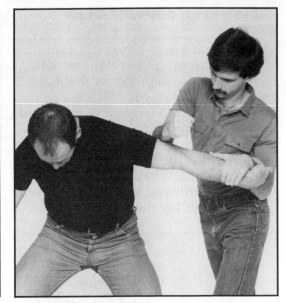

1. This escape is used when your left forearm is grabbed by your attacker's left hand (or your right by his right).
2. Move quickly up to your attacker.

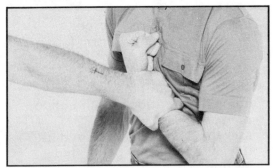

3. Make a fist with your grabbed hand.
4. Make a circular motion by moving your fist down and then up across your stomach until it touches your chest, so that the backs of his fingers are against your body.

5. Raise your other arm in the Defendo stance.
6. Twist from your waist to your left if he is grabbing your left forearm. This will expose his triceps.

7. At this point, you will be able to grab his left wrist with your left hand.
8. Keep his wrist close to you, which straightens his elbow.
9. Using the bony side of your free forearm, push or smash down against his triceps (for pain) or the back of his elbow (for injury), depending on the circumstances.

Relieving Painful Handshakes

Although heavy handshakes are often unintentionally painful, they are also sometimes used to intimidate and show off superior strength. You should get into the habit of keeping your fingers *slightly apart* when you stretch out your hand to meet a handshake.

If you forget to spread your fingers apart and to put your index finger on his wrist, try a more obvious method of breaking a heavy handshake. Relax

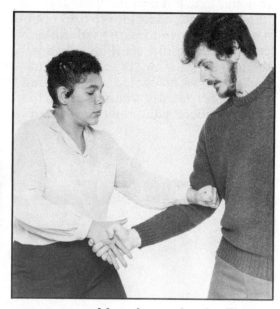

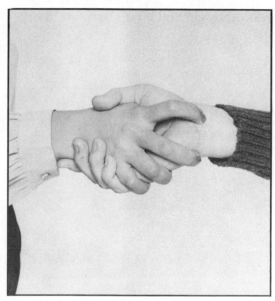

A startlingly effective yet barely noticeable method of eliminating the pain of a tight handshake is to stretch out your index finger and push down on the pulse in his wrist. If you don't believe this works, try asking your partner to squeeze your hand with *two* hands. Remember to spread your fingers slightly before shaking hands.

your captured hand completely. Then simultaneously strike the inside of his elbow joint with your free hand or forearm bone and pull your hand out of his loosened grasp.

Defending Yourself against Weapon Attacks

Although a weapon attack is very frightening, do not panic. Remember that you have two advantages over your assailant:

a) He is concentrating his strength on his weapon, so that if you minimize the effectiveness of the weapon, he has to rethink an attack strategy using his arms and feet.

b) He will assume that his weapon is a serious enough threat to stop you from using physical force. This overconfidence offers you the advantage of surprise. An exception would be the case of a drunk, drugged, or very nervous assailant, who may see every slight movement you make as an act of aggression.

Any weapon attack is very serious, and you should not attempt to block or remove the weapon unless you are sure that he is not just threatening but is going to use it against you. Try talking to your assailant to find out his motive, and give him any valuables you have immediately if he asks for them. If this attempt is unsuccessful and you have no choice but to defend yourself physically, you will need to have practiced your moves over and over again. Speed and accuracy are vital.

Try the gun attacks using a water pistol to check if your defense is quick enough to avoid getting shot, or, at the worst, receiving only powder burns. Use an empty paper-towel roll or a ruler instead of a knife to see if you would be grazed by a sharp weapon.

Blocking a down-thrust with a knife or similar weapon

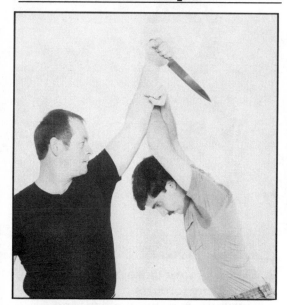

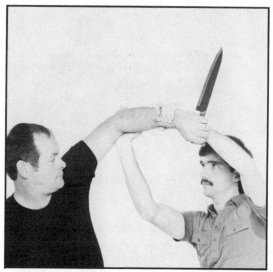

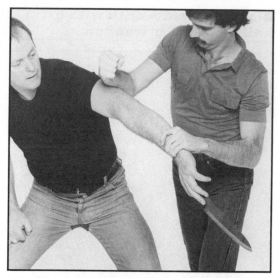

1. Assume the Defendo stance and get ready to block his arm in a manner similar to blocking a kick.
2. As the knife (or broken bottle, crowbar, or baseball bat) comes down towards you, lay one forearm flat on top of the other to make an "X".
3. Make fists and stiffen your forearms completely.
4. Lunge forward with your front foot to reach his arm sooner than he expects, and hit the fleshy side of his forearm with your crossed forearm bones. Tuck your head under your crossed arms so that the weapon won't hit your head if it falls free.

5. Grab his wrist with your left hand if he is striking with his left hand.
6. Turn his hand palm up, in the direction most awkward for him.
7. With your right hand, smash against the outside of his elbow joint to begin straightening it and bring it down in front of your body.

8. Continue pressure against his exposed elbow to straighten it completely.
9. While pulling his wrist up with your left hand so that he cannot bend his elbow, smash or push down with your right forearm on his triceps (which will cause pain) or the back of his elbow (which will cause injury).
10. If you meet any further resistance, hit a few other pressure points before escaping.
11. If the weapon has fallen near you, kick it far away or pick it up before escaping, unless this will seriously hinder your escape.

Blocking a side-slash with a knife or similar weapon

An assailant may try to intimidate you by waving a knife in front of you. Often — but not always — he may not know how to use his weapon, but believes it is intimidating enough to frighten you into submission. Only if you cannot talk your way out of this situation, and if your life is in danger, should you attempt to attack him.

1. Move back to avoid the knife as it comes in close to you, and assume the Defendo stance immediately.

2. Quickly move close again and use your bony forearm to smash forcefully against the exposed triceps of his knife arm. (Use your left forearm to strike his right triceps.)
3. Strike a few pressure points, such as the side of his knee and the floating rib.
4. Escape at this point, or else apply a hand grip (see *Grips*) until he falls and then restrain him (see *Restraints*).
5. If possible, stand on the knife when it falls and take it with you when you escape. Alternatively, kick it far away, or ignore it if it will impede your escape in any way.

Blocking a gun aimed within arm's reach

If the gunman is standing too far away, talk to him and act cowardly to give him the confidence to move closer.

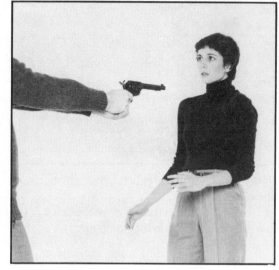

1. Keep talking to the gunman to distract his attention. Be ready to move suddenly in the middle of a word, when he is least expecting it.
2. He will not be alarmed if you raise both of your arms in the classic surrender response, "Don't shoot!", so *begin* raising *both* of them.

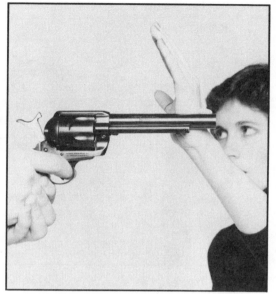

3. *On the way up,* suddenly hit the barrel (*not* his hand) outwards with the side of your left hand (if he is using his right hand), to deflect it away from you towards your left.
4. Simultaneously twist your body sideways to decrease your body area, in case the gun goes off.
5. Keep your eyes on the gunman.

□ *Common Error*
You must make this block while your arms are on the way up. It is too slow and dangerous to try *after* you have raised your arms.

6. As soon as the barrel is deflected, grab it with both of your hands and continue pushing it in its outward movement away from you in a *full* circle. This will lock his finger in the trigger and force his hand towards the back of his elbow, thus causing him to fall to the ground.
7. Strike or kick several pressure points.
8. You must get hold of the gun or kick it far away before you escape or restrain him.
9. You may receive powder burns, but if you do this move correctly you will not get shot.
10. If a companion of yours is standing near you on your left, try to move slowly away from him or her in a circle to the right, in case the gun goes off to the left when you hit it.

Blocking a gun pressed to your back or to the back of your head

If the gun is pointed below your shoulder level:

1. Raise your arms in a surrender position and keep talking to the gunman.

2. When he relaxes slightly, suddenly sweep down with either one of your arms. The direction is down towards your side and then across your back. This will deflect the gun.
3. Simultaneously twist your body towards the right if you used your right arm, to the left if you used your left arm. This will decrease the area in the gun's path, and add momentum to your sweep.
4. Strike a few pressure points.
5. Secure the gun and escape, or restrain him.

If the gun is pointed at your shoulders or above:

1. Raise your arms in a surrender position and keep talking.

Blocking a gun pressed against your chest or your stomach

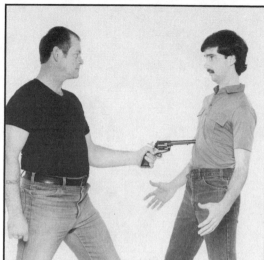

2. When he relaxes slightly or is distracted, suddenly bend your arms into the Defendo stance with tight fists and tensed muscles.
3. Simultaneously swing around forcefully, *keeping your arms in position*. Your forearm will deflect the gun.
4. Strike or kick several pressure points.
5. Secure the gun and escape, or restrain him.

1. Talk to the gunman as you *begin* raising your arms in "surrender."
2. *As you bring both arms up*, use your right hand (if he is holding the gun in his left) to deflect the gun away from you towards your left.

3. Twist your body sideways as you hit the gun, so that your side will be out of the way if it goes off.
4. Grab his gun-wrist and strike his nose, throat, or rib pressure points.
5. Secure the gun before escaping, or restrain him.

☐ *Common Error*
This block must be made while your arms are on the way up. It is too late to try it after your arms are already up.

Blocking a gun pressed to the side of your head

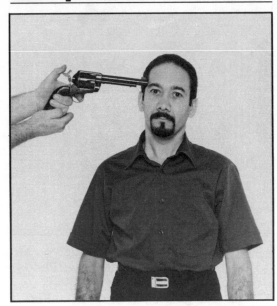

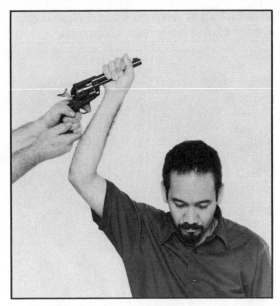

1. Keep talking to the gunman while you choose your moment.
2. Keep your arms ready at your side.

3. When he is slightly distracted, use your hand closest to the gun to move straight up suddenly. In one smooth, rapid motion, catch the gun and keep moving it upwards.
4. Simultaneously drop your head forward in case the gun goes off.
5. Slip your hand from his gun to his wrist and apply piercing pain by kicking the side of his knee and striking any other pressure points.
6. Secure the gun and escape, or restrain him.

Restraints

Most of the Defendo moves you have learned up to this point have been effective enough to knock your assailant to the ground and give you a chance to escape. However, you may choose not to escape, either because you wish to hold your assailant until the authorities arrive or because you are with a child or an elderly person who cannot run away with you. Under these circumstances, you should know how to restrain your opponent indefinitely. Use extreme caution in practice, as the restraints are very painful.

If you don't believe these simple restraints could stop an assailant from striking back or escaping, ask a friend to try them on you. If you make even the smallest move to retaliate or stand up, he should increase pressure.

Restraining an opponent who is lying on his stomach

This is the position he will be in after you have struck a triceps muscle, for example.

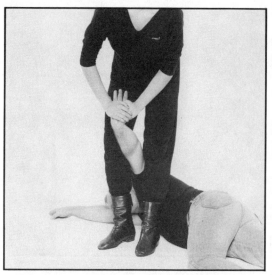

1. While he lies flat on his stomach, stand beside him.
2. Bring one of his arms straight up behind him, step across his arm so that you straddle it, and then clench it between your legs, as high as it will reach without excessive pain.
3. Grab his wrist and bend his hand down by placing your palms one on top of the other, at a right angle to his hand, across his *knuckles*.
4. Push his fingers down towards his forearm. (Use caution while practicing.)
5. Make sure his elbow is not bent.
6. If he resists or tries to escape, increase pressure on his wrist and force his arm towards his head. Twist his wrist towards the right if it is his left wrist. This added stress to the shoulder could break it.

Restraining an opponent who is lying on his back

An opponent will fall on his back after you have applied, for example, any of the *Hand Grips*.

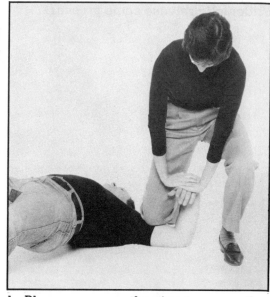

1. Place your assailant's triceps on the ground above his shoulder line.
2. Place your knee on his biceps. (Use caution while practicing.)
3. Place your palms one on top of the other, at a right angle to his hand, across his *knuckles*.
4. Push his fingers down towards his forearm, keeping his forearm vertical. His hip will lift off the floor if you apply enough pressure.
5. Keep pressure constant or increasing. Do not decrease, as the temporary relief will give him a surge of strength.

Turning your opponent over onto his stomach

Often your opponent will land on his back when you force or knock him to the ground. If it is necessary to restrain him for a long time, it is safer to move him over onto his stomach, where his ability to retaliate is slight, should you accidentally release some pressure.

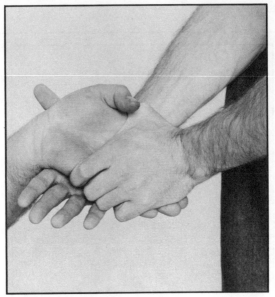

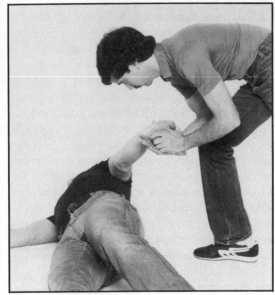

1. Keep hold of the hand you were gripping when he fell.
2. Pull it high into the air, thus straining his shoulder.
3. If you have hold of his left hand, use your left hand to turn his palm up. Place your fingers across his four fingers and squeeze tightly.
4. Rest the back of his wrist on a semicircle made by the thumb and forefinger of your right hand.

5. Using caution in practice, bend his fingers backwards with your left hand.
6. Keep his straight arm close to his body, so that his hand is about nine inches from his hip.
7. Still with the fingers down, push his arm into his shoulder joint. If you push it far enough, the pain will cause him to flip over onto his stomach.
8. Keep hold of his hand.